TROUBLE ON BOARD

TROUBLE ON BOARD

The Plight of International Seafarers

Paul K. Chapman

Introduction by Clifford B. Donn

ILR PRESS • ITHACA, NEW YORK

Cover and text design by Ann Lowe

Library of Congress Cataloging-in-Publication Data

Chapman, Paul K., 1931–
Trouble on board : the plight of international seafarers /
Paul K. Chapman; introduction by Clifford B. Donn.
p.   cm.
Includes bibliographical references and index.
ISBN 0–87546–180–8 (alk. paper): —
ISBN 0–87546–181–6 (pbk.: alk. paper):
1. Seamen.   2. Merchant marine.   3. Trade-unions—Merchant seamen.
4. Merchant seamen—Legal status, laws, etc.   5. Maritime law.
6. Shipping.   7. Quality of work life.   I. Title.
HD8039.S4C48   1992
333.7613875—dc20   91–31019

Copies may be ordered through bookstores or
directly from ILR Press

School of Industrial and Labor Relations
Cornell University
Ithaca, NY 14853–3901

Printed on acid-free paper in the
United States of America

5   4   3   2   1

TO GIGI

CONTENTS

PREFACE

O N JANUARY 24, 1985, the *Frusa,* an 11,715-gross-ton cargo freighter registered in Gibraltar, made an unscheduled visit to Bermuda for water and fuel. Normally they would have been taken on at an offshore bunkering buoy at St. George's without anyone leaving the ship, but foul weather prevented docking there and the ship was forced to pull into the docks in the inner harbor.

As the pilot was leaving, a seafarer bolted down the gangway before he could be stopped. On shore, the seafarer telephoned Ottiwell Simmons, the president of the Bermuda Industrial Union, a labor union that represents merchant mariners.

According to the seafarer, the crew on board had virtually been prisoners for the past four months and had been treated like "animals." He said the crew had been deprived of adequate water, had not been properly fed for the past fifteen days and were sick from the poor diet, and were owed four months' back pay. After investigating, Simmons told a reporter for the *Bermuda Royal Gazette,* "The captain was sailing around the oceans as if he had cattle instead of human beings aboard."[1]

The Yugoslav captain of the vessel made every effort to sail away before authorities in Bermuda could intervene, and the same day the ship pulled into port, he told the twenty-six Yugoslavian, Moroccan, and Sri Lankan crew members to cast off for Texas. When they flatly refused, he accused them of mutiny. The Bermuda port authorities sided with the crew.

Investigation revealed that the meat had been on board for ten months and was rotten. The canned food tins were rusty and had been bought after the expiration date. The port inspector, Ron Ross, estimated that there was only enough food for ten men for two days, yet the crew of twenty-six men had been ordered to depart for a destination several days away. There was only one tin of milk on board, and in the last port, Safi, Morocco, only sixty tons of water had been loaded, not nearly enough for an Atlantic crossing. According to the crew, "The taps were kept closed for four days after leaving port, and after that were opened only half an hour every two or three days." Later, Ross told me that there were no knives in the kitchen; a hacksaw blade with masking tape for a handle was used to cut bread.

Who owns such a ship? In this case, the owner remains anonymous. En route from Safi, it had been sold by Swiss Sea Shipping, Ltd., of Lugano, to Selsdon, Ltd., of Gibraltar. The new name was but a contraction of the old. The captain was ordered to paint out every other letter of the original name, *Fortunstar*, thus the name *Frusa*.

After their inspection, the Bermuda authorities declared the *Frusa* unseaworthy and held it until the new owner produced the proper certificates and it was adequately provisioned. Following heated discussion and threats of further legal action, members of the crew were paid back wages and were repatriated according to their wishes.

On August 4, 1991, a Greek cruise ship went down off the coast of South Africa. Although the press reported thatthe captain and some of the crew did not assist passengers in the evacuation, subsequent investigations revealed that many were very helpful, and some heroic, in effecting the rescue, in which no lives were lost despite heavy seas. The crew members lost all of their belongings as well as their jobs. Will they be compensated for their losses? Greek law provides for two months of extra pay in the case of shipwreck. Will the law be enforced for the crew from the Philippines, Mauritius, England, Hungary, Egypt, and the many other lands represented in the crew?

Who are the 1.2 million seafarers for whom the sea is their workplace? What laws protect them? Who enforces these laws? What recourse do they have if their employment agreement is broken? To whom can they turn? The answers to these questions point to the reasons conditions on board ships are sometimes nearly as primitive today as they were in earlier days of seafaring.

Seafarers who have been victimized, like those on the *Frusa*, frequently do not know where to turn. Many end up entrusting their problems to chaplains, especially if they have already spoken to the captain of the ship and the ship's agent to no avail. And contacting a maritime union could cost them their jobs.

As of 1988, there were welfare agencies and chaplains of many denominations in 895 ports around the world, working out of seafarers' clubs or visiting ships in port while using their parish church as a home base. They were practicing the ancient Jewish and Christian tradition of hospitality— welcoming the stranger in their midst.

For more than 150 years, chaplains have extended a welcoming hand to foreign seafarers, often with the hope of convincing them to convert to Christianity. More recently, they have extended their hands in friendship and service, knowing that the men and women working at sea are far from their families and communities and that life at sea is very difficult.

When a ship arrives in a strange port, dozens of people come aboard: bureaucrats of the host government, uniformed inspectors, agents for the shipowner, union representatives, salespeople, and prostitutes. It is the port chaplain whom the seafarer has learned to trust. It is the chaplain who is there to help the seafarer, offering assistance in placing a long-distance phone call home, converting currency at a fair rate of exchange, or getting to shops in town.

It is also the chaplain in whom a seafarer confides, for example, that the captain refuses to pay repatriation costs, as he is required, even though the seafarer's one-year contract ended six months ago. The seafarer wants desperately to go home but not at his own expense. The flight would cost the equivalent of two months' salary. According to his contract, he has earned the cost of his flight home; it is rightfully his

There have been major changes in seagoing life in the past two decades as a result of policy changes in the shipping industry. The time in port, for instance, has been greatly reduced. Some ships, such as container ships and car carriers, turn around in a few hours. In the past, the time in port would have been several days. Some tankers do not come into port at all but are off-loaded into pipelines or smaller tankers. Clifford Donn discusses these issues at greater length in the introduction.

The size of crews has also been cut, in many cases by as much as two-thirds. Automation on the bridge and in the engine room has meant that a ship can be operated by twelve to fifteen people, as opposed to thirty or forty in the past.

Wages have been greatly reduced as well. After a period of relative prosperity during and following World War II, the shipping industry suffered a serious recession in the 1970s, partly as a result of the fourfold increase in oil prices in 1973. To survive, shipowners left traditional ship registries in the industrialized world and registered their vessels in countries that did not require them to pay union wages or maintain Western standards. Increasingly, seafarers were recruited from poorer countries.

Living and working standards also deteriorated. Port chaplains frequently heard seafarers recount examples of abuse in the workplace. Without training and assistance, however, the chaplains could offer little more than sympathy. In response to this need, in 1981 the Seamen's Church Institute of New York and New Jersey established the Center for Seafarers' Rights with the approval of the International Christian Maritime Association, an organization of port chaplains worldwide.

Encouraged by the director of the Seamen's Church Institute, the Reverend James R. Whittemore, I became the director of the center. I had had some experience as a port chaplain and had heard my grandfather, who had been director of the Boston Baptist Seamen's Bethel, tell of nightly chapel services and of rescuing seafarers from the curse of alcohol. I had also spent many years working in the cause of social justice. Nonetheless, I was unprepared to tackle the problems of maritime employment.

Not surprisingly, as soon as the center announced its intentions—to "protect, empower and support merchant seafarers . . . by advocating for their basic human rights, confronting violations of those rights and improving national and international legal protections"—some industry and union officials questioned whether the church might be overstepping its authority. What right did it have to be meddling in the economic affairs of the maritime industry?

I was not dissuaded, however. The work of justice is an essential dimension of the life of the church.

The first step was to listen to seafarers describe their situations. I had heard only anecdotal reports from seafarers and chaplains of trouble on board. I now needed answers to specific questions: What were the most common problems, and how widespread were they? Were the seafarers' complaints rooted in serious problems on board, or were they merely the grumblings of disgruntled employees? Western mariners speak of "sea lawyers," colleagues who are quick to point out legal abuse. They were in no need of defense.

The International Transport Workers' Federation graciously welcomed me in their London office, where I read hundreds of letters from seafarers detailing their living and working conditions. Unpaid wages were the most common problem, followed by contract problems, followed by a series of problems—inadequate food, water, and accommodations; the use of unseaworthy ships; sickness and accidents; interpersonal conflicts; and problems with port authorities.

The Center for Seafarers' Rights prepared a problem report form, which was distributed to chaplains worldwide in the hope of developing an overall picture of the seafarers' situation. The cases that are described on the following pages are drawn from the sixteen hundred reports the center received between 1982 and 1990.

The next step was to determine what could be done about the problems seafarers were encountering. The staff of the center thus undertook to study the laws and regulations that apply on international ships. We employed a brilliant young lawyer, E. Welling Thomas, who spent several years researching the laws. Day after day, we offered help to seafarers who came or wrote to our office or whom we met on ships. The word quickly spread that help was available.

In the fall of 1981, I started writing a column called "Know Your Rights" for the *Sea*, a newspaper for seafarers published by the Missions to Seamen in London; 13,500 copies are distributed free of charge six times a year by seafarers' clubs around the world. The column is now regularly translated into Korean, Chinese, and Spanish and occasionally into Eastern European languages. It is also republished in Spain, the Netherlands, and the Philippines.

Unfortunately, the Center for Seafarers' Rights cannot always solve the problems it learns about. In 1985, for example, I received a letter in which the writer made the following comments: "They make me work for sixteen laborious hours, seven days a week, for negligible pay, and without any overtime allowances. My talents are being spoiled, my soul is being demoralized and my future is being driven into a complete dark." The seafarer described in detail the problems he faced. In this case we could not help, but we sent him a letter of encouragement, saying that we understood that the situation was very difficult, that unfathomable injustice exists in the world, and that we hoped the seafarer would take heart from knowing that people cared and were seeking to improve conditions.

There is increasing awareness among people in the shipping business—owners and their support staff, seafarers, and shoreside workers—that seafarers on some ships are abused and exploited, although there is disagreement over the percentage of ships on which there are problems. Some managers complain that the sea is already overregulated, that it should be free from all rules and social constraints. True, there is a confusion of laws and customs on the seas, but most are concerned with ship safety, pollution control, and navigation, not with the treatment of employees.

It is possible to operate a ship profitably while respecting the rights of the workers. Enlightened management honors the dignity of employees. In recognition of such managers, in 1988 the Center for Seafarers' Rights, in cooperation with the *Sea*, announced that it would present the Good Ship Award to any ship on which the seafarers felt they were being treated fairly. At least five crew members had to sign the nomination papers, and then a chaplain would investigate to confirm that the ship was well run and the crew was receiving fair treatment.

The *Bauchi* received the first Good Ship Award. Members of the crew considered themselves fortunate to have such good jobs; they received adequate pay; they were long-term employees of the shipping company, Torvald Klaveness & Co., which had established a pension plan and other benefits; families were permitted to sail; and food and accommodations were good. Barbecues and other special events were held on board. A magazine was published by Klaveness with news of workers on each of the company's ships. Most important, the management and officers respected everyone on board.

Those outside the maritime world are generally unaware of the importance of merchant shipping or of the underside of the industry. Ships, like storms, go "safely out to sea" and are quickly forgotten, yet they transport 95 percent of the world's international trade and are the primary medium for the international exchange of goods. Ships hold the international economy together, carrying billions of tons of cargo each year to thousands of ports.

When there is trouble in an industry as important as shipping, the world should know. I have written this book to let people know about the abuses and the exploitation of workers on today's merchant ships. All of the stories are true, and for every one I tell many more could have been told. In most cases I have omitted the names of the people involved, and occasionally I have changed the name of a ship or a seafarer to prevent reprisals or breaches of confidentiality.

In writing, I have often thought of Richard Henry Dana, Jr., whose preface to the first edition of *Two Years before the Mast* (1840) concludes:

> *If [this book] shall interest the general reader, and call more attention to the welfare of seamen or give any information as to their real condition which may serve to raise them in the rank of beings, . . . and diminish the hardships of their daily life, the end of its publication will be answered.*[2]

ACKNOWLEDGMENTS

I STARTED the research for this book at the Oceans Institute of Canada, welcomed by John Gratwick, Captain Edgar Gold, Cindy Lamson, Wade Elliott, Mary Brooks, and many others in Halifax. Research continued in London—at the offices of the International Transport Workers Federation; at the National Union of Seamen, where Jack Kinehan was most helpful; and at the National Union of Marine Aviation and Shipping Transport Officers (NUMAST), where John Newman and Andrew Livingston were very gracious.

I learned much in Manila from Captain Rogelio Morales and from the people who now make up the staff of the Maritime Education and Research Center, under the direction of Roli Talampas. I also want to pay tribute to Leo and Blanche Barnes of Bombay, whose studies of merchant seafarers have been of immense value.

American Baptist Women from churches across the land have also faithfully supported my work.

This book draws from the experience and sometimes the anguish of port chaplains throughout North America and around the world, who have struggled together to bring justice to seafarers. Some of the stories here have appeared in the *Sea*, whose editor, Gillian Ennis, has been very encouraging.

Many people have read and critiqued the manuscript in various stages—Julian Parker of the Nautical Institute, Richard Mulkern of the Missions to Seamen, Captain Colin Smith, Captain Michael Lloyd, Jim Martin, Richard Daschbach, Regine Harding, and Barbara Crafton.

I am indebted to Clifford Donn for writing the introduction, which puts what I have written in the broader economic context of the maritime industry.

The staff of the ILR Press deserves special praise. I am grateful to Erica Fox, the managing editor, for her interest and her extensive editing, which has greatly improved the book.

Most of all, the staff of the Seamen's Church Institute under the direction of Jim Whittemore warrants credit. Port chaplains—Francis Cho, Bob Montgomery, Cornish Espino, and Jean Smith—have contributed more than they realize. Although I wrote it, this book has been lived by the staff of the Center for Seafarers' Rights—Welling Thomas a decade ago and for six years Brother Pedro of Taizé, Jim Lafferty, and Mike Smith. We worked together on the cases that are reviewed here, discussing them at length and doing whatever we could to improve the living and working conditions of today's merchant seafarers.

I am grateful to all of these people and to the seafarers who have entrusted us with their problems and their lives. I hope this book contributes in some way to improving the plight of all seafarers.

INTRODUCTION

THIS book raises many issues concerning employment practices aboard commercial cargo vessels, especially "flag of convenience" ships employing so-called crews of convenience. The purpose of this introduction is to place some of these issues in their broader economic, legal, and social context.

Relatively little academic literature has been written in recent years about employment practices and labor-management relations in the international maritime industry.[1] One reason for this lack of attention in the United States is that dramatic postwar declines in the U.S. maritime industry have left the work force so small as to make it appear marginal relative to the overall work force in the nation. Another reason is that most scholars focus on domestic institutions, such as unions in their own countries, and the maritime industry is inherently international. Finally, those scholars who do focus on international issues typically concentrate on international bodies such as the International Labor Organization rather than on particular industries.

This lack of academic attention is a shame in that the growth of international economic interdependence has increased the importance of the maritime industry worldwide. Furthermore, there is much that can be learned from the maritime experience about industries in which there is almost unlimited potential for international competition.

THE ECOMOMIC ORGANIZATION
OF THE INDUSTRY

The commercial cargo maritime industry, the focus of *Trouble on Board*, essentially involves two groups: customers and producers. The customers, usually called shippers, are the people and companies with goods to transport. The producers, usually called carriers or operators, are the companies that operate the vessels that transport the goods.

Traditionally, the commercial cargo maritime industry has been divided into liners and bulk carriers. Liners, which are similar to common carriers in the trucking or railroad industries, follow fixed, published schedules and are willing to carry almost any cargo at published rates. A large container vessel is the prototype of the modern cargo liner.

Bulk carriers typically transport single cargoes for single shippers, using specialized vessels (tankers and ore carriers are examples). Accordingly, bulk carriers are sometimes referred to as contract carriers to differentiate them from liners (common carriers). Some products, such as automobiles, are now moved on what have come to be called neo-bulk carriers, however, and some bulk cargoes are carried in much the same fashion as liner cargoes. Wool, for example, is often shipped in containers. Thus the way the business is run, not the type of vessel used, determines whether or not a carrier is engaged in the liner or bulk service.

At first glance, the differences between liners and bulk carriers may seem small and not worth a great deal of attention. In fact, they operate so differently as to put them into almost entirely different industries.

Managing a liner involves dealing with regulatory authorities, marketing, consolidating cargos from different shippers, serving customers, and so on and is quite complex. As a result, the impact of on-board labor costs on the overall cost of the operation is comparatively small. In addition, most of the major international liners belong to liner conferences, essentially rate-setting cartels designed to protect operators from price competition. Most liner operators, including some who do not actually belong to the conferences, charge conference rates. There is therefore limited downward competitive pressure on costs, especially wage costs, in the liner trades.

The high fixed costs and low variable costs of the maritime industry make the existence of liner conferences important. Once a liner operator has invested in vessels and other essential capital equipment, has hired crews, and is committed to a regular schedule, it is relatively inexpensive to take on a bit more cargo when a ship is not full. In trades where liner conferences do not dominate, this high fixed cost/low variable cost economic structure results in price wars. Liner conferences are specifically designed to protect operators from such cutthroat competition.

Bulk operations are comparatively much simpler than liner operations. Elaborate marketing and regulatory activities are normally unnecessary. Accordingly, for many bulk shippers, such as petroleum and forest products companies, ocean shipping represents a very sizable percentage of their business expenses, much more than in the liner trade, and finding ways to reduce labor costs offers comparatively larger savings. Furthermore, the bulk trades have nothing equivalent to liner conferences, so there are fewer protections from price competition. Whether the companies contract with ocean carriers to transport their goods or operate their own vessels, there is thus a tremendous incentive to minimize the costs of ocean transportation. Labor is an obvious place to look for savings.

Most of the examples of abuse described in *Trouble on Board* occurred on bulk operations. Most involved bulk operators who were not tied to one shipper but who competed to secure cargoes from several shippers. This is distinct from shippers such as the Exxon Corporation in the United States, which controls a large fleet of its own oil tankers, or BHP in Australia, which maintains and operates its own fleet of ore carriers.

THE INDUSTRY IN THE
INTERNATIONAL ECONOMY

Since World War II, there has been a dramatic increase in the value of the goods and services being traded worldwide and in the percentage of total world output being traded. In the United States, the percentage of gross national product that is traded roughly doubled from 1970 to 1987.[2] The growth of world output combined with the growth in the fraction of that output that is traded has resulted in a tremendous growth in ocean shipping, the principal means by which goods are moved between nations.

Ocean shipping is also used to transport goods within countries, but domestic trade is regulated quite differently from international trade. The former is often limited largely or exclusively to vessels flying under the flag of the nation in which the vessel is registered. Such restrictions, called cabotage, place domestic maritime trade clearly and exclusively under the jurisdiction of a single nation.

Goods being traded between nations may be transported in several ways: in vessels of the exporting nation, in vessels of the importing nation, or in vessels flying under the flag of neither of these nations. Carrying goods between two nations neither of which is the country in which the vessel is registered is called cross trading. Both the fleets of traditional maritime nations (mostly industrialized nations) and of Third World countries face serious competition from low-cost cross traders.

To help newly industrialized nations develop their own flag fleets, the United Nations Conference on Trade and Development (UNCTAD) established an international liner code of conduct. Its basic aim is to reserve 40 percent of the trade between any two nations for the flag fleets of each of those nations. The remaining 20 percent is available for cross traders. Although a number of nations have adopted the UNCTAD Liner Code, the United States has not, and the U.S. government remains opposed to the code and to other similar cargo reservation arrangements. There is no equivalent code for the bulk trades.

In spite of the growth in international trade, the number of vessels has decreased since World War II, in large part because of two technological changes. First, oceangoing ships are dramatically larger, and, second, certain techniques are being used (especially containerization, roll-on/roll-off technology, and, to a lesser extent, barge-carrying technology) that significantly reduce the time it takes to unload and load in port. As a result, each vessel spends more time at sea and has a greater annual cargo-carrying capacity.

For a variety of reasons too sophisticated to analyze in detail, the larger and more complex vessels used today typically require much smaller crews than ships of the past.[3] In combination, the smaller crews and reduced time in port have affected the working conditions for seafarers by increasing their feelings of isolation, loneliness, and boredom.

Workers in all industries complain about wages and living conditions, but, unlike most shoreside workers, seafarers do not go home after a day of work. Because the employer provides not only work but also living accommodations and food, there is a much broader range of issues that can cause conflict.

FLAGS AND CREWS OF CONVENIENCE

The growth of world trade has led to a continuing search for ways to lower shipping costs, especially in the bulk trades. One might expect that sailing under one's own flag would offer advantages, but, in fact, costs naturally tend to be equal whether one sails under one's own flag or that of another nation. Costs are affected, however, by the policies of the nations with which one trades and the nation in which one's vessels are registered.[4] The message to vessel operators is clear: one way to reduce costs is to operate under the jurisdiction, or flag, of a nation that has minimal, inexpensive regulations rather than under the jurisdiction of a nation with a complex and costly regulatory framework.

In the past, vessel operators registered their ships in the countries where they lived, just as manufacturers tended to build their factories where they lived. The maritime industry is inherently international, however, and its employers began to think internationally earlier than shoreside employers did. While having one's factory next door may make managing a company easier, managing a vessel plying the Pacific trade routes is no easier because it happens to be flying the flag of the nation where the owner lives.

The ability to induce shipowners to register under one's flag enables a nation to raise revenue, much as the ability to attract shoreside industry does. The amounts of revenue generated may not seem large to most industrialized nations, but, given the limited sources of income of many Third World governments, it can be significant.

Open registries, or flags of convenience, have a long history.[5] Some of the earliest instances involved vessel owners who sailed under the flags of neutral countries as a way to avoid hostile actions during wartime. The growth of modern-day open registries is usually traced to the era of prohibition, between the first and second world wars. During that period, some U.S. owners registered their passenger vessels in Panama specifically so they could serve alcoholic beverages. Flag-of-convenience vessels were used again later, with the tacit blessing of the U.S. government, to circumvent neutrality laws and to provide military goods to the enemies of Nazi Germany before the United States formally entered World War II. After the war, the Liberian shipping code was designed by and for the benefit of U.S. shipowners and again had the tacit approval of the U.S. government.[6] Because of the dramatically reduced taxes required under the Liberian code, owners of excess U.S. tonnage were able to continue to operate profitably.

Vessels sailing under the flags of nations with open registries go by a variety of names, including convenient registries, flags of convenience, flags of necessity, and runaways. In the 1980s, they carried approximately half of all U.S. international waterborne commerce, more than ten times as much as the U.S.-flag fleet, and they completely dominated some trades, especially bulk operations such as petroleum shipping.

The number of nations attempting to attract foreign shipowners grew dramatically during the 1980s, and, increasingly, shipowners, especially from Greece, the United States, and Japan, registered with these nations.[7] Of the flag-of-convenience nations, Liberia and Panama had traditionally registered the largest number of vessels, carrying the most tonnage. They continue to register not only more than any other flag-of-convenience nation but any traditional nation as well. Growing competition among open registry nations has led to reductions in their already low levels of taxation on ship tonnage and to accusations that the registries are competing for business by promising laxer requirements during inspection and fewer regulations (and therefore lower safety standards for crews, the public, and the environment).

One of the principal costs of registering a vessel under a traditional registry is that most nations restrict hiring, at least in part, to their own nationals. The United States, for example, requires that all licensed officers and three-quarters of the unlicensed crew on U.S.-flag vessels be U.S. citizens. In the industrialized nations, high standards of living on shore and often powerful maritime labor unions make hiring such crews many times more expensive than hiring crews from the Third World. Savings from hiring cheaper crews are particularly attractive to owners of vessels in the bulk trades, which are more competitive and in which labor costs represent a large percentage of the operating budget.

One of the primary ways in which flag-of-convenience nations tempt vessel owners away from their national registries is by allowing the owners to hire crews from wherever they wish. These crews of convenience, as they are called, typically consist of seafarers who share neither the nationality of the flag under which the vessel is sailing nor the nationality of the vessel's owner. Technically, crews of convenience can be found on "national" flag vessels, but in practice flags of convenience and crews of convenience often go together and in combination result in many of the worst abuses endured by seafarers.

The importance of crews of convenience has grown dramatically, as reflected in the shift in the composition of the world's seafarers, from 15 percent Asians in 1960 to 67 percent in 1987.[8] The Philippines, South Korea, India, and Indonesia have increasingly become major suppliers of seafarers, largely to flag of convenience vessels. As Chapman discusses in this book, crewing agents in these and other nations have gone into the business of supplying low-cost crews to vessel operators.

Crews of convenience typically work for very low wages compared to seafarers from developed nations, and they are often forbidden by their terms of hire to complain about their living or working conditions to foreign authorities or labor unions or to join or form a trade union. Winning a victory in a foreign port occasionally brings compensation for poor conditions aboard ship, but the gains are often extremely short-lived, for as soon as the vessel returns to international waters, the seafarers are often fired or blacklisted. Jobs available to Third World seafarers are often far better than those available in their home countries, so many seafarers are loath to complain or contact authorities, even when confronted with exploitation.

As *Trouble on Board* makes clear, crews of convenience are thus easy targets for unscrupulous shipowners. The stories that fill this book document just such exploitation, including failure to pay agreed-upon wages, failure to pay any wages at all, and failure to provide decent living conditions. The conditions Chapman describes are so offensive as to make one think he must be writing about an earlier era, not the second half of the twentieth century.

The International Transport Workers' Federation (ITF) has attempted to resolve some of the seafarers' problems. An international trade secretariat, the ITF is affiliated with the International Confederation of Free Trade Unions and brings together representatives of non-Communist transportation trade unions from around the world. The ITF has long waged a campaign aimed at forcing operators of flag-of-convenience vessels to sign collective bargaining agreements with representative national unions or to bargain with the ITF itself and enroll all of their crew members in the ITF Special Seafarers' Department.[9] Vessels without legitimate collective bargaining agreements or ITF "blue certificates" are frequently boycotted in ports around the world where the ITF is particularly active, such as Scandinavia and Australia.[10] ITF port inspectors talk to crew members and require vessel masters to produce pay records as well as evidence of ITF or other collective bargaining agreements. As in the cases of the seafarers whose stories Chapman tells, action often results only when exploited crew members are desperate enough to seek help.

Trouble on Board focuses on cases that have come to the attention of port chaplains, and, as such, may underplay the role of the ITF and its campaign to aid exploited seafarers. There is a difference, however, between the role of port chaplains and the role of the ITF. Ultimately, if the ITF were successful, flag-of-convenience vessels would no longer exist and the crews of "national" flag vessels would be unionized in the registering nation, which would be the home nation of the vessel owner.

Unionization is the key here. When the ITF finds that a vessel has no legitimate collective bargaining agreement, it tries to force the operator to accept an ITF agreement that includes, inter alia, enrolling all crew members in the ITF Special Seafarers' Department and paying dues for all of them.

Port chaplains do not necessarily hold any brief for trade unions. The chaplains' only goal is to resolve seemingly legitimate complaints and end exploitation or abuse that comes to their attention.

Unions in such traditional maritime nations as the United States, Britain, and France object in principle to flags and crews of convenience, but clearly not all operators of such vessels are engaged in inhumane or unethical conduct. In fact, many are quite reputable. At the same time, given the level of fear among crew members, the fact that most flag-of-convenience vessels clear port with no complaints is not a reliable indicator that crews are being treated fairly. In most cases, crew-of-convenience seafarers who contact a port chaplain or an ITF inspector should expect that they will never work as seafarers again. Thus, only the most exploited and most desperate will complain. Accordingly, Chapman's accounts may involve some of the worst cases of exploitation, but they also clearly involve the proverbial tip of the iceberg.

As Chapman discusses, over the years international bodies have attempted to regulate the conditions on flag-of-convenience vessels. Most of these efforts have not been successful.

International organizations have also attempted to set minimum employment standards for seafarers. The International Labor Organization (ILO), originally an agency of the League of Nations and now an agency of the United Nations, has been involved in this issue for most of this century. Indeed, approximately half of the international labor conferences the ILO has held have focused primarily on maritime employment. The minimum standards the ILO recommends are extremely low compared to standards of industrialized countries, but, as Chapman's account points out, many carriers violate even these standards. The mechanisms available to enforce the ILO's standards are weak or nonexistent.[11]

The ILO's standards are meant to apply to all seafarers. The problem is that, despite the lobbying efforts of various national and international trade union bodies, international law basically does not recognize the concept of the flag of convenience. According to international law, the nationality of a vessel is that of its flag state and is not related to the nationality of its owners or crew. Various union bodies have lobbied and continue to lobby to require vessel owners to register their ships in the nation in which the owners live, thereby establishing a "genuine link" between the flag of the vessel and the nationality of the owner. On occasion, the union bodies have succeeded in convincing international regulatory bodies to adopt the "genuine link" terminology, but overall unions have had little success in placing meaningful limits on open registries.[12] Indeed, the U.S. government has supported and continues to support open registries (to the detriment of its own flag) by treating many flag-of-convenience vessels owned by U.S. citizens as available for use in national emergencies (that is, under "effective U.S. control").

RELEVANCE OF *TROUBLE ON BOARD* TO THE AMERICAN INDUSTRY

In recent years, U.S. media discussion of the maritime industry has focused on oil spills. Following the March 1989 oil spill by the *Exxon Valdez*, the media addressed such issues as the need for double hulls, the size of the crew (the *Exxon Valdez* had a crew of nineteen at the time of the accident), and substance abuse by crew members (the master of the vessel was alleged to have been drinking at the time of the incident), although liability for the cleanup at times dominated discussion in general-circulation newspapers and magazines.

The issues surrounding the *Exxon Valdez* are far removed from those Chapman raises. The *Exxon Valdez* was a U.S.-flag vessel with a crew of U.S. citizens. Federal law, the so-called Jones Act, requires that vessels carrying cargo between U.S. ports sail under the U.S. flag. This "Jones Act fleet," together with vessels operating under subsidy contract with the U.S. Maritime Administration, make up the bulk of the U.S. ocean-going fleet. Most of the rest of the fleet is largely dependent on indirect subsidies (carriage of military or agricultural-aid cargoes, some of which are reserved for the U.S. fleet). All such vessels are subject to a variety of laws, regulations, and safety inspections by the Coast Guard, and almost all have contracts with trade unions. These contracts cover all sea-farers on board up to and including the masters. This combination of conditions makes the exploitative situations Chapman describes virtually unheard of on vessels in the U.S.-flag fleet.

This does not mean that Chapman's story is of no concern to Americans. Indeed, the issues he discusses affect the United States in a variety of ways. First, the exploitation Chapman documents takes place in U.S. territorial waters and ports. American courts are often asked to provide relief by arresting the vessel in question and effecting compliance with agreements or international regulations. Recent changes in international law have given the government of the port state (the nation where the vessel is in port) increased authority and responsibility for the maintenance of safety standards and other internationally agreed-upon regulations for all vessels of whatever flag happen to be in its ports.

Second, U.S. citizens own a large number of flag-of-convenience vessels. At least some of the owners responsible for the evils depicted in *Trouble on Board* are undoubtedly Americans who are not content with avoiding U.S. taxation and paying U.S. wage rates and are trying to save even more money by mistreating or cheating their crews.

Third, the U.S.-flag fleet has declined in relative importance throughout the postwar period. The U.S. fleet has lost and continues to lose especially in competition with flag-of-convenience operators. The competitive advantage of flag-of-convenience operators is further enhanced to the extent that they can successfully cheat or mistreat their seafarers. There are valid arguments over whether the use of flags and crews of convenience constitutes "unfair competition," but there is little argument that failing to pay seafarers agreed-upon wages or to provide them with decent food and accommodations is an unethical way to compete.

There are no effective mechanisms available either to national governments or international agencies for regulating vessel operators engaged in unscrupulous competition. Until there are, port chaplains like Paul Chapman will continue to have a litany of horror stories to recite.

CLIFFORD B. DONN

TROUBLE
ON BOARD

ONE

The Sea as a Workplace

USTY leatherbound volumes in maritime libraries and museums throughout the Western world record in gruesome detail the living and working conditions aboard merchant ships in the eighteenth and nineteenth centuries. Diaries, journals, novels, court records, and historical studies provide a comprehensive picture of the abuses seafarers suffered in the past.[1] The diary *Two Years before the Mast* by Richard Henry Dana, Jr., in which he recorded his voyage of 1834–36 on the *Pilgrim* and the *Alert*, is perhaps the most famous of these documents. Dana, a Harvard University student on leave to cure an eye disease, was so moved by the abysmal lot of common seafarers that he dedicated his life as a lawyer to improving their plight.

Dana's book describes accommodations that were dank if not outright wet and repeated instances of seafarers who had inadequate food and drink: "Our fresh provisions were, of course, gone, and the captain had stopped our rice, so we had nothing but salt beef and salt pork throughout the week with the exception of a very small duff on Sunday."[2] Sicknesses, the most notorious of which was scurvy, were common.

3

He tells of the dangers of the profession and in scorching detail of violence and cruelty to seafarers on ships and ashore. A flogging inflicted by Captain Frank Thompson on two shipmates alarmed Dana profoundly: "As [the captain] went on, his passion increased, and he danced about the deck, calling out as he swung the rope, 'If you want to know what I flog you for, I'll tell you. It's because I like to do it! Because I like to do it. It suits me! That's what I do it for!' "[3]

Many diaries from the nineteenth century tell of similar cruelty. At the young age of twenty, Samuel Samuels was serving as chief mate on the *Catherine* under a captain known as Bully Edwards, a man who "would rather see a fight than eat his dinner."[4] One night in Holland, the rough crew became violent. The Dutch authorities pressed charges against the ringleader, Jack, an Englishman. Jack hid in the fo'c'sle, but he was pursued there by the Dutch authorities, whom he resisted with knives. Finally he was brought out swathed in blood. Samuels continues as follows:

> *After being secured he was taken on board the guard ship and double-ironed and a guard was placed over him. The following morning he was tried by a court-martial and condemned to be dipped and to receive three dozen lashes. . . . Directly after the sentence had been pronounced he was taken to the port gangway. He was then placed on a grating, stripped to the waist, head and body bent down, with his thumbs fastened to the pin-rail, and he thus received his first dozen lashes. The crew then ran him up to the yard, whence he was dropped overboard, striking the bottom in his descent. They then took him on board, the second dozen were given him, and he was again run up to the yard and dropped. After the third dose he was carried below in a fainting condition to be washed in pickle.*[5]

Since flogging was outlawed long ago, one might well assume that the working environment on modern ships is neither so cruel nor so primitive. Would that that were so. Sadly, many of today's seafarers are being abused mentally and physically under conditions reminiscent of those Dana and Samuels described.

A chaplain in Taiwan tells of ships that leave from Kaohsiung with no dedicated living facilities for the crew members on board. They simply curl up and sleep where they can. Because there is no operating galley, rice is cooked over a charcoal fire on deck. And as the following letter, addressed to the Center for Seafarers' Rights, indicates, even corporal punishment is still practiced, although in a less bestial form than on the *Catherine*: "We embarked at Port Louis, Mauritius, to the Indian Ocean, contracted for six months for one trip. During hard working days for just small mistakes, the officers kicked, punched and beat us to blood."

Conflicts are inevitable when people from a variety of cultures are brought together in the same workplace. But when officers or managers deliberately take unfair advantage of these workers' economic or social vulnerability, because they are from other cultures, it is exploitation—a form of violence.

In 1984, at anchorage in Puntarenas, Costa Rica, a Filipino bosun, Willi Sanchez, struck and killed his Norwegian first mate. Sanchez had been aboard the ship for the previous nine months and had shown no signs of a violent temper. He appeared to be cooperative and pleasant, despite palpable tensions on board, which a chaplain in Brooklyn, New York, had noticed the previous month.

In the trial that followed, witnesses attested that the first mate had incessantly taunted Sanchez but, consistent with his upbringing, the seafarer had ignored the provocations. Finally he had lost control under the pressure and struck the chief mate. The cultural difference between the two men is important. Two people from the same culture may have been able to find a way of reconciling their differences.

Two United Nations–related international agencies are concerned with ship operations. The International Maritime Organization (IMO), located in London, addresses issues of safety, pollution, and navigation. The International Labor

Organization (ILO), located in Geneva, addresses labor problems. The IMO is concerned exclusively with maritime matters. The ILO is concerned with labor conditions in all workplaces, including the sea.

Cargo ships that are built today must conform to standards established by the IMO and the ILO. There are limits, for example, on the level of engine noise and vibration in the crew's accommodations and requirements regarding heating, cooling, ventilation, and sanitation. In addition, the crew must have comfortable living facilities and space set aside for them if they are sick or injured.

Unless a ship is properly maintained, it rather quickly becomes a hazard. Salt air and water can destroy today's steel ships, and vessels deteriorate rapidly if they are not carefully maintained. It is possible to protect aging steel with fresh paint, but it is also not uncommon to see an eight-year-old ship that looks ready for the scrapyard. Liberia, which registers more ship tonnage than any other country in the world, will not register a vessel that is more than twenty years old unless a waiver is granted.

Ships that are deteriorating are often sold for far less than a new ship would cost. And, unfortunately, the new owners are not likely to spend the money required to return older vessels to prime condition. After a couple of years, many are sold again in worse shape. A ship that is still operating after twenty years has often changed hands three or four times. Rust covers the crew's quarters, the paneling is broken, the doors and portholes will not close, the toilets and sinks are stopped, the generator frequently fails, and the water is cloudy. The hatch covers leak. The overall message is that the owners do not care.

Captain Philip Cheek in *Legacies of Peril* describes a voyage from Israel to the Baltic Sea in which his vessel, the *Tiger Bay*, broke down so often that a trip that should have taken two weeks at most required three months. Cheek relinquished the command in protest; later, the ship went aground and was lost because of faulty navigation equipment. One can imagine what the crew's quarters were like if the other equipment on the ship was so deficient.

In February 1981, seventeen men from a ship that carried bulk cargo came to my office to report their situation. They were embarrassed by their misfortune, but the conditions aboard ship had become intolerable. Despite subfreezing temperatures, there was no heat in the crew's cabins and consequently no running water or plumbing. The generators were not working, so there was no electricity for refrigeration or illumination. The galley was inoperable, and at night the ship was like a ghostly tomb, lit only by a few flashlight beams in the crew's quarters.

Two months earlier the members of the crew had arrived in New York from Central America, expecting to sail within a few days. They had received the little information they had from their recruiting agent in Puerto Cortes, Honduras. When they arrived in New York they were met by a man who called himself the chief engineer and who brought them by van to the ship. They described their feelings when they finally saw their ship; the excitement and anticipation of a new job quickly turned to apprehension. They were appalled by its condition.

They were determined to make the best of a bad situation and immediately went to work making the ship seaworthy. But there was far more to be done than they could manage. Supplies were slow to arrive. Food, which was cooked on an open fire on the rear deck, was often in short supply. And, although they had expected to be paid at the end of the first month, they still had no money at the end of the second. After two more weeks, when the temperature had not gone above freezing, they were quite demoralized and ready to take action, whatever that might be.

On questioning, they were not sure of the name of the vessel. Their letter of employment agreement listed it as the *Sealift*, but there was no name on either the bow or the stern.

When I asked to see their employment contract, they said they had none—only a letter of employment agreement, which did not specify the terms of the work. Further, there was no indication where, or if, the ship was registered. It had once been registered in Liberia as the *Opel*, but the registration had expired and the seafarers did not know where it was currently registered. The Greek engineer who served as their foreman claimed he did not know where the ship was registered and that he too was receiving shoddy treatment from the agent who was his boss. He claimed not to know the name of the owner.

Besides their intolerable working conditions, the Hondurans were in legal limbo. By now their transit visas to the United States had expired. They had worked for two months without pay, leaving them seriously in debt at home. They had no money to buy airline tickets home, and they did not wish to give up their employment. Fortunately, the Seamen's Church Institute was able to accommodate the men in a hotel it operated while a colleague and I pursued their case.

We were continually frustrated in our attempts to take legal action. There was some indication that the ship was registered in the Cayman Islands. If this were so, the seafarers were under the authority of Grand Cayman, but there was no one at the consular offices for the Cayman Islands or the United Kingdom who would accept responsibility. Because it was a foreign ship, U.S. officials assumed no authority. They claimed it was strictly up to the consul of the registering country to set matters straight. The U.S. Coast Guard would step in only if the ship sought clearance to sail and was found unseaworthy. The U.S. Public Health authorities would intervene only if there were rats on board, and then they would contract for "deratification" of the ship. It was mid-winter; there were no rats. Ensuring that the crew had food, water, and heat was not part of the mandate of the U.S. Public Health Service.

We could find no one who would accept responsibility. Although everyone involved suspected that the so-called chief engineer was the owner, there was no evidence of this, and hence he could not be held responsible.

In effect, the Hondurans were victims of complete deception. They thought they would be sailing but in fact had been brought to the United States, with the promise of meager wages, to repair the ship. The owner was obviously in over his head and could not manage even with the "cheap" work crew.

Having pursued every legal avenue to no avail, the Center for Seafarers' Rights paid for the crew to be repatriated, using its own funds. The ship was eventually towed away, presumably to be sold for scrap. In July 1987, however, one of the chaplains of the Seamen's Church Institute reported that he saw the same ship, now called the *Anna T*, in port at Staten Island, New York. The new crew members were complaining that they had not been paid in months, the ship was inoperable, and they were being required to repair it. The same story.

This case is obviously an extreme one, but it is not unusual.[6] Because it was one of my first cases involving a crew in a U.S. port, I wondered whether there were really so few laws that protected foreign seafarers or whether I simply did not know about them because of my inexperience. I checked with a number of admiralty lawyers, but they readily admitted that their cases involved ships and cargo, insurance, and charters and that unless a seafarer had been injured, it was not profitable for them to bother representing members of the crew. They were not familiar with the plaintiffs' side of the law.

A problem somewhat similar to that of the *Opel* arose in April 1986 on the *Brant Point*, registered in the Cayman Islands. A Canadian crew was flown to Ipswich, England, from Nova Scotia, Canada, only to find the ship in deplorable condition. The crew set to work to make it seaworthy, but, as in the case of the *Opel*, the seafarers could not do all the work themselves and they were not being paid for their efforts. When waterfront authorities declared the vessel unseaworthy, the owner telexed the ship and accused the crew of being at fault. Calling the seafarers strikers, he reminded them of their situation: "You have agreed when you joined vessel to accept state and conditions of vessel; also you entered into an agreement by signing shipping articles. . . . I understand when you joined vessel that you were prepared to work, assist, etc., in getting the vessel in comfortable conditions."

The owner went on to say he had done all he intended to do to make the ship seaworthy except replace the smoke detectors and the first-aid kit. The rest was up to the crew. If the crew continued to report deficiencies to the authorities, the owner said, he would not be able to operate. If the seafarers were going to be obstinate, they should probably leave the ship and get themselves home. At the time this threat was made, the crew had already gone for more than a month without pay. The seafarers did leave but not until they secured legal assistance so they could make a claim for the unpaid wages.

The situations described above occurred on cargo ships, but they could just as well have occurred on cruise ships. The only major difference between them is the purpose of the voyage and sometimes their economic viability. The rapid growth of the cruise ship industry during the 1980s contrasted markedly with the depression in the cargo industry. It was one bright corner in the dark maritime world.

Until thirty years ago, passenger ships carried "human cargo" from one port to another. Today, they operate as luxurious entertainment hotels, some catering to an upper-class market, others to middle-class vacationers.

Many of the former passenger liners—Cunard, P. & O., and Holland America—successfully made the transition from the liner business to the leisure business, and the crews aboard continued to work under adequate conditions. Meanwhile, new cruise companies were buying older passenger liners forced out of business by transatlantic airlines, refurbishing them, and marketing them to middle-class Americans.

Traditional Norwegian maritime companies have made Miami the "cruise capital of the world." It is now the headquarters for ships making one-, three-, and four-day or longer Caribbean cruises costing as little as one hundred dollars a day, complete. The availability of cheap labor from the Caribbean, Central America, and Asia is one of the keys to the profitability of this undertaking. It takes little or no experience to work on the staff of a cruise ship. The concessionaires who run the casinos, the food service, the sleeping rooms, and the laundry can recruit crews from anywhere in the world where labor is cheap. One commonly used strategy is to hire crew members of thirty-five or forty different nationalities, thus avoiding the danger that a crew will join together to protest the working conditions.

Advertisements that imply that the workers and passengers enjoy similar conditions easily entice young people to the glamorous world of luxury cruising, and workers are tempted by the promise of big tips. Waiters who have good stations with full passenger loads *can* make very good tips, but the base salary is very low—as little as fifty-two dollars a month.[7] Furthermore, the kitchen help, cleaners, sanitation help, and laundry workers receive no tips at all.

As the following letter illustrates, even waiters often receive no tips:

> As a waiter on cruise ships I am forced to convince passengers to write on comment cards that the food was excellent and the service. The results go to travel agents. Because of the competition, the companies are doing this in order to inform the agencies that they are a good company. To do this the waiters are harassed mentally.
>
> Each week waiters with the less points are demoted for a week and work as busboys or serve the officers without getting tips. The contract does not refer to these demotions. Since we get $52 a month plus tips, when we serve the officers as punishment, that is all we get.
>
> Example: A waiter can be an excellent waiter. But for some reason on that cruise by the time he goes to the kitchen they

run out of chicken. He'll make some passengers unhappy or the food is not of the passengers' liking. Or for some reason the kitchen is behind and the waiter has to wait for food and if it comes out late he can get poor marks. Even if he received only two "good" marks and all the rest were "excellent" but all the other waiters got only excellent he would be demoted. We have to tell the passengers to put excellent.

Ships that were designed primarily to move passengers efficiently and comfortably from point A to point B must now provide luxurious amenities, necessitating far more workers. The number of crew members has doubled, but the crew's quarters remain basically the same, straining the ship's capacity past safe and comfortable limits.

I have been aboard cruise ships on which eight and ten crew members bunked in a tiny room. In one case, a seafarer had no room and had to carry a mattress into a companionway when he wanted to sleep. In another case, two seafarers on different shifts were assigned to the same bunk. The toilet and shower facilities were so overused they were often clogged and putrid. The crew's dining room seated only sixty people, although the crew numbered several hundred, and was ugly and dirty. A heating table to keep food warm for latecomers did not work; nor did a refrigerator for milk and other beverages. The dining room also served as the crew's only recreation area. A sign on a locked cabinet, which was painted closed, read "Crew's Library." A small black and white television, which operated only in port, was apparently the only recreational outlet.

The crew is not allowed in the passenger areas except on business. Unauthorized socializing with passengers is grounds for immediate dismissal. In addition, crew members are often fined by their superiors without knowing why. The contrast between the overindulged passengers and the restricted crew is at times almost unbearable.

In 1983, a young Barbadian college student told me about the working conditions he had endured on a cruise ship earlier that year. He had been a wiper in the engine room, where he had worked for twelve hours a day, seven days a week. The room in which he worked was hot and noisy. On several occasions he had been badly burned when he was required to clean out a boiler that had not sufficiently cooled. Although there was a doctor on board for the passengers, he was not allowed to see him. There was no relief from the work— no recreational outlets, not even a deck where he could walk in the open air. He had virtually no direct contact with the officers in charge. He was given orders in almost military fashion, and he obeyed them.

He was appalled by the way wastes were discharged; tons of garbage were thrown overboard, often in sight of land. Two seafarers worked full time—at night—disposing of garbage. Effluents were pumped directly into the sea, even when the ship was in a harbor.

In January 1984, as a result of many such reports, the Center for Seafarers' Rights sponsored a conference on the working conditions of seafarers on cruise ships. During the course of the conference, the differences among cruise companies became obvious. The Norwegian companies, whose workers were protected by union contracts, had gone to some lengths to provide their crews with congenial work environments. The management of one company had contracted with the Work Research Institute in Oslo to study ways to improve the conditions. The rights of all workers were protected, and there were adequate ways to make complaints and to redress grievances. By contrast, the management style of some of the other companies was paternalistic and arbitrary, and there were no contracts. In chapter 3, I discuss the significance of these practices.

As a result of the Miami conference, the staff of the Center for Seafarers' Rights was invited by the management of the Chandris Line and the Carnival Cruise Line to investigate employment conditions. On the Chandris ship the *Britanis*, which was registered in Panama, we heard frequent complaints that the food was inadequate. We ate alternately with passengers and crew. In contrast to the lavish meals the passengers were given, the crew received no more than meager rations, invariably a nondescript stew. There was not enough space for the crew to eat, and many stood or sat on the stairway or on boxes in the hallway above.

When we reported our findings to the captain of the *Britanis*, he told us that Chandris was not responsible, that they contracted the crew's mess to a hotel and food caterer and that the ship was paying eight dollars a day for the crew's food, which was enough for a healthful diet. He then showed us the crew's menu, which was included in the contract with the caterer.

We copied the menu and posted it on the wall of the seafarers' dining room and asked them to compare what they were given to eat with what they were supposed to be given. The quality of the food improved at once. For breakfast the next morning the crew was given a choice of coffee, tea, or cocoa and eggs or dry cereal in addition to their normal oatmeal. There were not enough forks or spoons, and those who did not bring their own had to eat with their fingers. The captain claimed the crew members had stolen the utensils. When we suggested that the crew could use plastic forks or spoons, he announced that plastic was not good enough— it had to be stainless or nothing.

For a few weeks the crew apparently ate quite well, but subsequently the staff reported that the quality of the food deteriorated as soon as our investigation ended. Our investigation revealed that the caterers on the *Britanis* were cheating the crew in other ways, all of which we reported to Chandris to no avail. The cost for a soda was marked up 100 percent, for instance, although the maximum allowed by the caterer's contract with Chandris was 10 percent.

Accommodations for the crew on the *Britanis* were substandard by any measure. The ship, which was almost sixty years old, was built for far fewer workers. The seafarers slept on triple-level bunks, eight or ten in some cabins, and were provided no storage area. Books and clothing were stacked at the foot of the bunks. One bare bulb lit the entire cabin and was being turned on and off all day and all night as the occupants went to and from their duties. The cabin had no ventilation and smelled like a gymnasium locker room.

The toilet facilities were also repulsive. International standards on new ships call for one shower for every eight people on board and one wash basin for every six. The filthy, broken showers and toilets on the *Britanis* were used by many more.

We made suggestions for improvements, some of which were accepted, but they were followed only during our investigation. When there is no way to enforce minimum standards, management can be as shoddy as it wants. And when unemployment is high, as it is in the Caribbean, Central America, and several countries in Asia, a seafarer's complaint often leads not to improvement but to dismissal, as we shall see.

The conditions for women on cruise ships is no better than it is for men. Until the maritime recession in the mid–1970s, increasing numbers of women joined the crews of cargo ships, at all levels, especially on ships from Scandinavia, Greece, and Eastern Europe. Since then, the number has diminished, but women are still on the hotel staff of cruise ships and typically represent up to 20 percent of the total crew. As this letter from an American illustrates, however, the living and working conditions for these women can be very trying:

> When Catherine and I boarded the Victoria *to begin our new jobs as cocktail waitresses, we weren't prepared for what was ahead. The bar manager introduced himself and showed us our "accommodations." The accommodations turned out to be a small room with a bed, a sink, bare light bulb, one electrical outlet, a wardrobe, and a chest of drawers. My mattress had a spring that was sticking out. There was a shower down the hall for us that we shared with two men. It was always kept padlocked, and it took us two days to get the key. . . . It was the pits. I'll never know why they bothered to lock it. It was musty, moldy with peeling paint and human waste coming up through the drain. It made me sick. If this is how they treat*

women, how do they treat the poor men? I'm afraid to find out.

I could go on about other things on the Victoria, *but they are only what I heard, and I prefer to stick with what I saw and what I experienced. I do not lie or exaggerate as there is no need to in this case.*

There was a time in maritime history, before the structure of the industry became so hierarchical, when all seafarers on board a ship had a voice in its operation. A worker's income often depended on the income from the voyage. In some cases, wages were a percentage of earnings. In the Acts of the Apostles, from the first century, there is evidence that the crew was consulted before a ship left port.[8] And a maritime law from about A.D. 1300, called the Laws of Oleron, contained a requirement that the captain consult the crew before making a decision relating to the operation of the ship. The captain had to ask, before sailing, "Gentlemen, what think you of this wind?"

> *If any of them see that it is not settled, and advise him to stay until it is, and the others on the contrary would have him make use of it as fair, he ought to follow the advice of the majority. . . . It is a general sea law that a master of a ship shall never sail out of port, never weigh or drop anchor, cut masts or cable, or indeed do anything of consequence, let him be in whatever danger may happen, without the advice of the major part of his company. . . . He must call all together to consult.[9]*

More recently, a few companies have sought to include the members of the crew in the decision-making process. The dignity of workers is enhanced when they do not simply take orders but are given decision-making responsibility. Such respect for the opinions of the workers is unfortunately rare in the maritime workplace. Most decisions are made by corporate headquarters. The well-being of the workers is generally disregarded except as a means of increasing productivity.

With some notable exceptions, there is very little evidence

that humans are regarded as a significant component of the maritime enterprise. Human creativity and potential are generally disregarded. Each ship represents a huge investment of capital—cargo ships can cost up to $100 million and cruise ships even more—yet little attention is paid to the people entrusted with their operation. "Hands" are hired at the lowest rate and regarded as disposable parts.

Outside the restraints of national and social control, the shipping industry, like other transnational industries, runs the danger of operating for no other reason than to make profits—preferably short-term profits that provide a quick return on investments. People are but a means to this end. If the industry has no other motivation but profits, no consideration of human values, or moral responsibility, or world view that respects the environment and deals fairly with the public, the working conditions on board ships will continue to reflect this poverty of values.

Many seafarers have signed on expecting, and trusting, that they will live decent lives on board and that their human dignity will be respected. Many have been sadly disappointed.

TWO
Getting a Job

FOR centuries, life aboard ship was so abhorrent that shipowners resorted to extreme methods of recruitment. Ancient mariners were often slaves, prisoners, criminals, or religious rebels who were chained for years with an iron collar that allowed them neither to stand erect nor lie down.

In the seventeenth century, Sir Walter Raleigh noted that since the food and other conditions aboard ship were so terrible, workers went only grudgingly, as if they were to be "slaves in the galleys."[1] Recruiting agents, called press gangs, virtually kidnapped workers, often using violent methods, in return for a fee paid by the government. The English lived in fear of these recruiters, who roamed the waterfront and the countryside, shanghaiing crews and dragging them aboard.

In the eighteenth century, shadowy figures called spirits enticed unsuspecting country people to ships by promising them great wages and often by giving them cash advances.[2] The tactics of the maritime recruiters were so reprehensible that pamphleteers urged abolitionist William Wilberforce "to stop worrying about black slaves and take a look at what was happening at home."[3]

Not surprisingly, crews often deserted at the first opportunity, especially in the New World. "Crimps," in league
with boardinghouse keepers, came aboard arriving vessels and
enticed crews to desert, using the promise of a lively time
ashore and a better job aboard another ship in the future.[4]
The crimps terrorized the waterfront and maintained a stran-
glehold on the seafarers' employment, yet legislation to abol-
ish their activities failed because the shipowners depended
on the crimps for crews even if they disapproved of their
tactics.

In some places sailors organized to protest their exploitation. In 1934, for example, the Marine Workers Industrial
Union created the Centralized Shipping Bureau in Baltimore.
All mariners shipping out of the city were hired through the
bureau, on a rotating basis. Citing the need for the bureau,
Harry Alexander, chair of the committee that established it,
claimed shipping agents were the most ruthless of all the
parasites preying on seafarers.

> These shipping agents . . . are given the power by shipowners to
> dictate to the seamen as to who is to go on a certain job. . . .
> These crimps are not satisfied with what they are getting from
> the shipowners for shipping men. They have various sidelines.
> Most of them have rooming houses where they charge the seamen
> from three to five dollars a week and then in some cases put
> from three to six in a room. Others have cheap restaurants
> where the seamen have to pay first class prices for third class
> food; some have clothing stores where they are forced to pay
> thirty five to forty dollars for a suit of clothes, for which any
> decent place would charge fifteen to sixteen dollars; and then
> there are some who have saloons either in their name or somebody
> else's where the seamen are forced to spend their money in
> order to get a job.[5]

Crimps were infamous for cheating seafarers. They would
routinely go aboard arriving vessels before the seafarers got
paid and entice them into boardinghouses where the costs
of liquor and women soon exceeded the wages from their
last voyage. In debt to the boardinghouse keeper, the seafarers

now had no choice but to accept the employment the crimp arranged. If the seafarer returned to the port at the end of his next voyage, the crimp would claim he was owed for debts incurred during the previous visit.

In spite of all the trouble the crimps caused, sailors saw them as their allies, as their kind of people. Many of the crimps were former sailors, and some returned to sea from time to time. Often, seafarers and crimps stood side by side against the common enemy—the high-class shipowners, masters, and others in authority.

Strong-arm recruitment methods lasted well into the twentieth century and serve as an indictment of the working conditions aboard ships. If the ship had been a more attractive and just workplace, workers would have sought the seagoing life. As it was, they were dragged on board, generation after generation.

The methods used to hire seafarers was one of the first issues addressed by the International Labor Organization following the Peace of Versailles in 1918. ILO Convention No. 9, the Placing of Seamen Convention, says that "the business of finding employment for seamen shall not be carried on by any person, company or other agency as a commercial enterprise for pecuniary gain; nor shall any fees be charged directly or indirectly by any person, company or other agency, for finding employment for seamen on any ship." Thirty-one nations have ratified the convention, thus incorporating the terms into their own national bodies of law, but only rarely is the law enforced. Recruitment methods still cause seafarers great difficulties today.

Today's recruitment problems vary in their severity depending on the number of trained and experienced seafarers who are available to work the ships. When seafarers are in demand, recruiters generally offer decent terms. When there are more seafarers than jobs, recruiters tend to take advantage of the seafarers who are available. There is no orderly international system for matching labor supply and demand.

There was a great demand for Western seafarers to transport troops and war supplies during the two world wars, and terms of employment were good. Soon after World War I, jobs became scarce and merchant mariners either left the sea altogether or found they had to wait longer and longer for low-paying jobs.

Shipping remained strong after World War II until the recession of the 1970s. At about that time, recruiters began hiring increasing numbers of crews from poorer countries for low salaries, leaving many skilled mariners without work. Many found jobs ashore or retired. Maritime schools in the West fell on hard times because there were few career opportunities for seafarers after graduation.

Bypassing higher-salaried officers in favor of lower-paid workers has created a major problem for the industry. A 1990 study conducted by the University of Warwick, England, indicated that there is now a shortage of as many as fifty thousand officers and that the figure will reach four hundred thousand by the year 2000. To overcome this problem of their own making, recruiters will be forced to pay more money to entice officers back to sea and to encourage young people to enter maritime schools. Ensuring that ships have competent crews is more than a matter of training; captains, for example, must have years of experience before they are ready to take command of a merchant vessel.

Economic conditions in countries supplying labor also affect the supply of seafarers. As the standard of living rose in Korea in the 1980s, for instance, Korean seafarers found they could make more money at home than at sea, and the number of Korean seafarers dropped from fifty-one thousand to forty-one thousand from 1985 to 1989.

The opposite situation exists in the People's Republic of China, which for some years has been training men to be seafarers. If China were to implement an aggressive policy to place these hundreds of thousands of trained mariners on international ships, the worldwide recruitment situation would be radically altered. The labor market was similarly affected during 1989 and 1990, when Eastern Europe was being opened up to the West and Russian, Polish, Yugoslavian, and other Eastern European seafarers sought jobs, many for low wages, on international ships.

Fraudulent recruitment practices continue to plague the industry, and in spite of ILO Convention No. 9, many seafarers and shipowners are still charged recruitment fees. Job seekers from countries with high unemployment rates, deceived by the myth that there are high-paying jobs at sea, are easy victims of corrupt recruiters. Greece, for example, has ratified ILO No. 9, but on Akti Maouli, the busiest street in Piraeus, dozens of employment officers ply their trade by means reminiscent of those used in the sailortowns of the New World one hundred years ago. Young men from dozens of Southern Hemisphere countries have come to Greece to find work, knowing that the country has one of the world's largest registered fleets. Corruption is rampant, and jobs are often given to the highest bidders, so that the majority of seafarers go home empty-handed, having spent their money and all their patience living on the streets of Piraeus.

The hiring situation in Asia is also very difficult, as the following example illustrates. The seafarer who told me this story had waited for months for his job.

> When they finally tell you about a job, it's always rush, rush. You have to leave in two days. They bring you into the office for a briefing and make you sign that you won't complain to a union. And there are all sorts of papers to sign, and forms to fill out. It costs five dollars for this and ten dollars for that. They are making money all the time. I signed so many blank papers. I was too busy and too excited to ask questions.
>
> We met the Flag Anna in Italy, and the job was okay. It's a scrap ship so we have several days in port while she is loading. The trouble came on our first payday last week in Newark. All of us had a deduction from our pay slip of one hundred dollars for "company business." The crew who have been here for a while says it happens every month. I asked the captain, who

told me it was a standard employment agency policy. Nothing could be done about it.

Later, when I phoned my wife, she said the recruiting agent told her there would be no allotment payment this month. [An allotment is the portion of a seafarer's salary that goes directly to his family.] $450 was being withheld as a recruitment fee. They are taking everything we earn.

For many years the Philippines has been the world's largest supplier of maritime labor. High unemployment has forced increasing numbers of Filipino workers to go abroad to find work—construction workers to the Middle East, entertainers to Japan, nurses to the United States, housemaids to Hong Kong, and seafarers worldwide. Like other Asians, Filipino seafarers have been working on foreign-owned ships for centuries.

In 1974, President Ferdinand Marcos formalized the hiring process by creating the National Seamen's Board. (It has since become part of the Philippine Overseas Employment Administration [POEA].) The stated goals were to establish and maintain a comprehensive training program for seafarers, to provide them with free placement services, to obtain the best possible terms and conditions of employment, to secure full implementation of seafarers' employment contracts, to maintain a complete registry of all seafarers, and to regulate the activities of shipping company agents in hiring seafarers for overseas employment.

The unstated goals were at least as important: to promote and develop employment opportunities abroad through a comprehensive marketing strategy and to promote the hiring of Filipinos in groups, as well as through government-to-government arrangements. In 1982, President Marcos described the goals as follows: "For us overseas employment addresses major problems: unemployment and the balance of payments position."[6]

Clearly, the primary goal of the POEA is to find more and more shipowners who will hire Filipinos. When protecting the rights of the seafarer and protecting the job come in conflict, rights are invariably sacrificed. In 1985, for example, all personnel on board ships owned or managed by Hanseatic Shipping Company of Cyprus received a letter from Crescencio Siddayao, the deputy administrator and officer in charge of the POEA, indicating that he had approved a request from Hanseatic for an immediate pay reduction, even though the workers had a contract. Rather than challenge the right of the employer to cut wages mid-contract, the POEA approved the cut to save the jobs. The seafarers were advised they could accept the cut or leave. Appeal was not an option.

To ensure that money earned abroad returns to the Philippines, the government requires that Filipino seafarers send 80 percent of their wages to their home country, where the foreign currency is exchanged into pesos and deposited in the account of an allottee designated by the seafarer.

There is no question that the POEA has been successful both in finding seafarers jobs abroad and in collecting foreign exchange payments. Each year from 1982 to 1985, an average of 391,000 overseas workers, including seafarers and employees in land-based jobs, remitted $3.1 billion in payments to the Philippines. According to the Central Bank, in 1988 overseas workers remitted $857 million into the Philippine economy, 12 percent of the country's total earnings from exports. Overseas workers are now the country's number-one export, having overtaken semi-conductors.[7]

Once the Philippine government established the overseas employment program and it was evident that workers were making more money abroad than they could at home, thousands of ambitious Filipino entrepreneurs were eager to cash in on the bonanza. Many people have thus benefited from the relatively higher salaries Filipinos are making overseas.

Recruiting agencies top the list of groups that have profited. The original intention was that the Philippine government would function as the placement agency for all overseas workers. Toward that end, in 1975 the Ministry of Labor and Employment published a labor code that included a provision that outlawed private profit-making employment agencies. The new law was consistent with official internationally accepted maritime policy and with the terms of ILO Convention No. 9.

The private sector objected to the government serving as the sole employment agency, however, and in 1978 Presidential Decree 1412 was passed, which removed all restrictions on private recruiters. Soon private agencies had taken over the majority of the "head-hunting" business.

Federal agencies have also benefited from the large number of seafarers being sent abroad. Filipino seafarers must deal with at least thirteen federal agencies, many of which charge them fees to qualify for overseas employment. Typically, seafarers must purchase a professional license (deck or engine) from the Professional Regulation Commission ($3.00); a seafarer's record book from the Philippine Coast Guard ($2.40), a passport from the Department of Foreign Affairs ($25.00); and a registration card from the POEA ($.75 or $1.50 if laminated). In addition, they must receive clearance from the National Bureau of Investigation ($2.00) and from the police ($1.00). They must also pay for medical and dental examinations, including psychological testing ($12.50), and for vaccinations from the Bureau of Quarantine ($1.00) and provide the recruiting agent with photos ($2.50) and photocopies of various documents ($5.00).

Recruits who will be working on a ship that is registered in a country where they are not licensed may also be required to purchase licenses. The license for Filipino officers seeking work on a Panamanian flagship is $335, for example, and $145 for crew.

The number of recruiting agencies in the Philippines has proliferated dramatically. In 1990, there were three hundred private maritime recruiting agencies that enlisted Filipino workers and in cooperation with the POEA sought out employment opportunities for them abroad. The decision of the Marcos regime to allow private recruiting agencies has resulted in a phenomenal growth in the number of seafarers who are placed. The agencies have mounted an aggressive worldwide campaign, in close cooperation with the government, to convince shipowners to use their services. A change in Norwegian policy, which allows non-Norwegians to work on Norwegian-flag ships, combined with a preference among Norwegians for Filipino crews, accounts for some of the recent increase in employment. In 1989, 115,000 POEA-processed seafarers were placed, an all-time high, and at least 5,000 more bypassed the POEA completely and were hired directly. By comparison, only 23,500 were placed in 1975.

More than fifty maritime schools, some sponsored by recruiting agencies, turn out as many as 10,000 Filipino graduates a year, and 230,000 Filipino seafarers are registered with the POEA. The competence of these graduates is another matter. Many of the schools offer very inadequate instruction, yet many graduates have the impression that they are well trained and ready for service at sea. Many will never be hired because they lack skills and experience.

It is common to see a cluster of Filipino men and some women waiting near a recruiting agency, hoping that jobs for which they signed up will become available. The majority of these men and women are natives of the provinces and therefore forced to move to Manila or other population centers while they wait. Many resort to sleeping in parks during the months, even years, that they must wait for a possible job. To ingratiate the recruiting agents, some serve as their personal servants during the waiting period. They run errands, drive the agent's car, clean the house, whatever it takes to curry favor and increase their chances of getting hired when the right job comes along.

Finding a job is both difficult and expensive for these workers. Many are advised to offer an under-the-table payment to the recruiting agent to increase their chances of securing employment. In 1986, the International Christian Maritime Association, an umbrella organization for maritime church and welfare agencies in 895 ports worldwide, conducted a survey of 1,376 Filipino seafarers. Thirty-eight percent (522) admitted to having paid an illegal recruitment fee. Corrupt agents also pad the fees seafarers are required to pay for passports and other documents, and some require seafarers to pay performance bonds of up to a thousand dollars as a guarantee that they will fulfill the terms of their contracts.

Most seafarers have to borrow money to pay these fees. According to a 1983 study conducted by the Integrated Research Center of De la Salle University of Manila, the average overseas worker under contract invested thousands of pesos to get his or her job and often had to work for months to break even.

To compete with recruiters in other labor-supplying countries, Filipino recruiting agents offer shipowners an attractive package: a low recruiting fee and in some cases no fee at all (all costs are passed on to the seafarers); absolute assurance that the seafarers will not be involved in union activities while they work for the owner; a promise that the seafarers will work hard and be docile (there are serious reprisals for those who complain); and a relatively low salary scale, currently $286 per month for an able-bodied seafarer. The rate of pay is suggested by the International Labor Organization. According to some contracts, seafarers are paid overtime in addition to their base pay of $286. Other seafarers receive $230 or $240 a month as base pay and a fixed amount for overtime, regardless of how many hours of overtime are worked, bringing the total pay to $286.

A 1985 survey conducted by the Center for Seafarers' Rights of seventy-five government-licensed Filipino recruiting agents found that shipowners are charged agency fees of six thousand to thirty-six thousand dollars per year for a ship with a crew of twenty-five seafarers (nine officers and sixteen crew). Most agencies charge the shipowner an initial processing fee and then a monthly fee, plus out-of-pocket expenses for office supplies. The monthly fee for the term of the contract is calculated in a great variety of ways. It is often a percentage of the allotment due the seafarer's family. One agency surveyed admitted that it keeps 5 percent of a seafarer's allotment as a service fee. Others indicated that one way or another the seafarers are charged a percentage of the recruiting fees.

The primary concern of the recruiting agent, like that of the POEA, is to find seafarers jobs, not to protect their rights. The following letter to a shipowner from the president of a Manila recruiting agency underscores the agent's concerns.

> *Filipino seamen recruited by us are required to execute an Affidavit of Undertakings refraining them from joining or communicating with any local or foreign unions or associations of any country. Any slight violations thereof by the seaman shall mean outright dismissal, forfeiture of his remaining wages, cancellation of his seaman certificates and all costs of repatriation shall be to the seaman's account. Therefore the interests of the shipowners are protected.*

The Philippine government is well aware of the corruption within the recruiting industry. In 1979, the Philippine Task Force on Illegal Recruitment cited 1,479 cases of illegal and fraudulent recruitment practices: charging workers illegal fees, forcing workers to sign double and triple contracts, sending workers to jobs that did not exist, and so on. The actual number of cases of fraud is thought to be higher than the number reported. Workers who consider reporting incidents of cheating are silenced by the threat of unemployment.

In an effort to improve the situation, approximately fifty recruiting agents at a Manila conference in December 1987, sponsored by the International Christian Maritime Association, adopted a voluntary Code of Good Employment Practice. Franklin Drilon, labor secretary of the Philippines, who was at the conference, identified many practices that were counter to maritime protocol, including collecting extra fees and requiring seafarers to pay their airfare to meet a ship. In enumerating the problems, Drilon noted that some recruiting agencies

> *accept substandard shipboard conditions of employment for seafarers even when they violate international conventions con-*

cerning safety standards. There are occasions when seafarers were left stranded in foreign ports without support from agencies. Many agencies have cheated their seafarers by short-changing allotments of the seafarers' household through the use of lower foreign exchange rates. Some agencies have failed to pay the allotments altogether despite having received the amounts from the shipowners.

Cronyism often threatens attempts to eliminate corruption. The chief of the POEA told me that he revoked the license of one corrupt recruiting agency on three separate occasions and that in each case someone higher in the bureaucracy reinstated the company within hours. The Philippine Task Force on Illegal Recruitment suspends up to thirty recruiters' licenses each week, but rarely is a license permanently cancelled.

Unfortunately, the Philippines does not have a monopoly on corruption. The following story describes the situation in Taiwan.

> Slick agents from Kaohsiung go into the villages and lure young boys, often fourteen to fifteen years old, to go to sea. They buy them clothes, food and alcohol. These young people don't realize that they must pay them back.
>
> The agents are very clever; they promise the boys a way to make the big money. They introduce them to a very "safe" and "well-equipped" ship. This is how many tribal boys become fishermen.
>
> What they don't know is that they will be charged as much as a thousand dollars in introduction fees. Often, the parents' signatures are forged so that their children go to sea without their knowledge or permission. These youths know nothing about contracts, wages or the dangers of the sea. They don't know how to swim and are inexperienced with machinery. When they return from a voyage, usually between one or two years in length, what little profits due them are then reclaimed by the fishing company as payment for the fees it says it has given to the agent. Of course, the introduction agencies and fishing companies are conspiring together to defraud these young workers.[8]

Recruiting agents throughout the Third World use deceptive advertising to help lure unsuspecting job seekers. In August 1987, for example, the *Singapore Strait Times* printed an advertisement announcing that there were "well-paid opportunities on luxury cruise ships." The ad said that previous experience was not essential, that salaries ranged from seventeen thousand to thirty thousand dollars annually, and that the workers would live in "modern cabins with luxury food."

To learn more about these employment opportunities, the interested party had to pay thirty-nine dollars. In exchange for the payment, he or she received a booklet that showed pictures of ships and gave addresses of cruise companies. Applicants who succeeded in getting a job had to pay additional fees, in monthly installments.

The worst abuse a recruiting agent can perpetrate is to send a worker to a job that does not exist. Seafarers arrive in foreign ports with documents, telexes supposedly from shipowners, and letters of agreement only to discover that the arrangement is a fiction. In August 1986, a Bangladeshi electrician, Jamal Jabara, and a Ghanian second engineer, Josiah Uddin, arrived in New Orleans, having been sent by a man who identified himself as the chairman of Bolastra (Bolivian-Asian-Trading). Each had already paid $1,741 for airfare and consular papers. They had also paid $12 each for taxi fares in New Orleans and $200 each to the chairman of Bolastra for placement fees, for a total of $1,953 each.

Jabara and Uddin had a letter from the chairman of Bolastra to a ship's agent in New Orleans, who, as it turned out, had been out of business for some time. The letter introduced the two men and said they were to join the *Santa Cruz*.

Lost in New Orleans, the two seafarers were taken to the seafarers' agency, where Chaplain Elmo Romagosa investigated. After five attempts to reach the chairman of Bolastra, who lived in the YMCA in Singapore, the chaplain was told that the *Santa Cruz* was delayed in Mexico. Further investigation revealed there was no such vessel. The whole undertaking was a scam.

The two seafarers had nothing to show for their $1,953 each and were now penniless in New Orleans. The only way they could return home was to be deported at the expense of the U.S. Immigration and Naturalization Service. Ships carrying seafarers who have been deported may not enter the country from which they were deported unless a security guard is posted on board to ensure that the seafarers do not go ashore. To avoid this expense, ships almost never hire deported seafarers. The only way for the seafarer to clear the record is to pay the deportation costs. Having borrowed two thousand dollars each to get their jobs, Jabara and Uddin saw no possibility of paying the costs of deportation, especially without jobs at sea. Their careers had been ruined.

All too many seafarers have fallen victim to such deception. The files at the Seamen's Church Institute document many instances in which alleged recruiting agents in Callao, Peru; Colombo, Sri Lanka; Piraeus, Greece; and Manila, Philippines sent seafarers to nonexistent jobs.

An even more common abuse is to promise seafarers nonexistent terms of employment. I met Mario at the Stella Maris Seamen's Club in Miami. He was twenty-four years old, had a degree in hotel management, and had been working in the kitchen of the Manila Hotel. Having already received several promotions, he was optimistic about his future career. Someone had advised him that if he worked on a cruise ship, his chances of finding a better job would be greatly improved. After speaking to several recruiting agents, one told him that the cruise ship *Carnivale* was looking for an assistant maitre d'. Mario had to borrow deeply to pay the required fees and for his airplane ticket from Manila to Miami, but he was confident he would soon make back the money in salary and tips. He had been "guaranteed" a minimum of a thousand dollars a month.

In Miami, Mario presented himself to the staff of the *Carnivale*, who knew nothing about a job opening for an assistant maitre d'. After a brief discussion with the staff and a futile attempt to contact the recruiting agent in Manila,

Mario accepted a job as a pot washer for $240 a month. With no money to fly home and no possibility of paying off his debts in Manila, he had no choice. It would be months before he would break even and return home.

Mario's story is not unique. Seafarers often find that the conditions on board ship are not as attractive as the recruiter said they would be. Liberty Manning Agency of Manila signed up four Filipino entertainers to work on a luxury cruise ship, the *Bermuda Star*, which at the time was cruising back and forth from Bermuda to New York City. They were shown pictures of passengers' cabins, which they were told would be their accommodations, and one was assured that he would be able to adhere to a Muslim diet. They were also told they would be given a contract to sign on board and that the ship's agent would meet them at Kennedy Airport in New York and drive them to the ship.

When the entertainers arrived at Kennedy Airport, they were unable to find the agent, and the New York office for the *Bermuda Star* knew nothing of his whereabouts. Undeterred, the four bought tickets to Bermuda, where the ship was to be docked the next day. There were indeed jobs for them there but for much less money than they had been told, and they would have to work a longer workweek. In fact, they finished their first day of work at 4:00 A.M. and had to report to work again at 9:00 the same morning. They had no contract, and the accommodations were very unpleasant. The officers laughed when one entertainer said he had been promised a Muslim diet.

A week later, the four were in my office, having jumped ship in New York. They were hoping to return to the Philippines.

In many cases, seafarers view their recruiting agent, not the captain or the shipowner, as their employer. The agent becomes the seafarers' patron, someone to whom they remain loyal despite the abuses. The others in authority are strangers; seafarers often do not know the shipowner, and the officers who give day-to-day orders are often from another country and speak another language. It is the agent with whom the seafarers negotiate the terms of their contract, in whose office employment agreements are signed, and the person who forwards allotment payments to their families. It is the agent who orients the seafarers to the responsibilities of their new job. On board, seafarers sometimes wear T-shirts or coveralls with the recruiting agency's name and insignia.

In some cases, shipowners employ a single agency that is responsible for every aspect of the ship's operation, from recruiting, to obtaining cargo, to financing. In other cases, these responsibilities are divided among a number of agencies. But even shipowners who perform some of these functions themselves usually hide their identities behind a corporate veil, using an agency name rather than their own. Reading Lloyd's *List of Shipowners* one could conclude that shipowners are "managers only." Human contact is with the agent.

Because various layers of bureaucrats protect the shipowner, pinning responsibility when something goes wrong can be very complicated. Consider the case of the *Gogo Regent*. Arriving in Boston in July 1987 from the Persian Gulf, where the ship had been hit by rockets during the Iran-Iraq War, the members of the crew phoned their families in Korea, with the help of Chaplain Jim Lindgren and the staff of the New England Seamen's Mission. Their families, they learned, were not receiving allotment payments. The seafarers were already tense as a result of their experience in the gulf. Discovering that they were not being fully compensated for their dangerous and hard work on board was more than they could tolerate.

The crew immediately stopped working. The Norwegian captain retaliated by locking the galley, denying the men any food. He quickly repatriated one member of the crew, whom he thought was the ringleader, and had the local police arrest two other crew members for insubordination. Since it was the weekend, all the grocery stores near the port were closed, and the crew had no food for two days.

My wife, the Reverend Regine Harding, and I were passing

through Boston at the time, and Jim Lindgren persuaded us to help him with this problem. We decided that Regine, who had worked as a port chaplain, would go to the ship and talk with the captain.

The presence of a woman in the previously all-male environment had a calming effect. As she approached the captain, whiskey tumbler in hand, he rose gallantly from his desk and welcomed her. He then proceeded to explain his side of the story.

Meanwhile, I attempted to contact the shipowner, the registry, the recruiting agent in Korea, and the media. We had calculated that public exposure of the situation would hasten a solution. We were right; the news media jumped on the case. "No Food, No Wages for Gogo Regent's Korean Crew" read the headlines in one Boston newspaper. On reading this, Korean-American residents in the Boston area immediately offered to help. Korean restaurants brought food. Korean lawyers volunteered to represent the crew. The Korean-American Society of New England contacted the recruiting agent in Korea. Many Koreans came to the ship to offer encouragement.

We were not sure who was responsible for the seafarers' plight. The owner of record claimed he had sent the wages to the Korean recruiting agent; he in turn claimed he had not received any money; the captain accused the recruiting agent of gambling the money away. Liberia, the registering country, sided with the owner and in an official report of the incident put the blame on the Korean agent.

In response to the negative publicity, and to get the ship sailing again, the owner sent the seafarers what he claimed was a second wage payment. He also paid repatriation costs for those who wished to return to Korea.

We tended to agree with the Liberian investigation that the Korean recruiter was the cause of the scandal until three months later when members of a Yugoslavian replacement crew put a lien on the Gogo Regent in Sweden because they were not being paid. This new evidence suggests that the shipowner and not the Korean recruiting agent may have defaulted. Our records show that the same owner had also seriously delayed paying the Filipino crew of a small cruise ship he operated off the coast of California.

A Korean third engineer subsequently told me that the manager of the recruiting agency had been tried in court in South Korea and had served six months in jail for having taken the allotment money and invested it in another business. It is obviously difficult to ascribe responsibility in such a drama when the primary players claim to be taking orders from others who have the real authority.

Andrew Guest, writing in *Seatrade* in 1988, sums up the problem:

> A cowboy ship manager, well-known in the trade for ridiculously, suicidally low rates, wins a contract from the desperate or greedy owner and then cuts corners, skimps on maintenance, buys cheap second-hand stores and does deals with chandlers, ship repairers and manning agents. Backhanders, "profit" sharing on discounts, are salted away while the ship turns to rust and the mixed-nationality Third World crew wait for their pay.[9]

The union hiring hall is one of the most significant advances organized maritime labor has won in this century. When a union member is ready to look for a job, he or she registers with the union and is assigned a priority based on seniority and other objective criteria. As jobs become available, union members submit their cards for the jobs that interest them. The top-priority applicant gets the job. While favoritism and fees may not be eliminated, the hiring hall is an improvement over the recruiting agency.

Unfortunately, very few of the world's maritime jobs are posted in union halls. Most job placement is still arranged by recruiters. It appears that anyone who wishes—in the Philippines, in Honduras, in Taiwan, in South Korea, and in many other countries—can hang out a shingle announcing "Crews for Sale." And there are always marginal shipowners from all the continents who will select a crew based on who will accept the lowest wages rather than on the applicants' experience or the quality of their work.

In port cities around the world, from Miami, Florida, where more seafarers are employed than in any other American city, to Colombo, Sri Lanka, crews of the world's merchant fleets are being recruited at great profit to recruiting agents. We have researched the situation in Puerto Cortes, Honduras, where there are ten recruiting agents; two, perhaps three, treat their seafarers fairly. The rest are taking advantage of the high rate of unemployment, and all of them are making kickback deals with potential employers, none of which benefit the seafarers.

What choices do seafarers have when they are in direct competition with other seafarers who are willing, for the sake of a job, to accept poor terms? Most of the maritime employment agencies in Honduras, for example, call themselves unions (*syndicats*), but like many maritime unions in the Third World, they are privately owned businesses that do not function democratically. Their "members" have no vote; they have simply applied for jobs through the unions and are either working or waiting for work.

THREE
Employment Injustices

BROTHER PEDRO, while on the staff of the Center for Seafarers' Rights, observed seafarers being hired in the port of Bridgetown, Barbados, while he was on board the cruise ship the *Victoria*. As the ship came into port in the early morning, he noticed a line of men and women standing on the dock. No passengers were scheduled to be boarded in Barbados, and at first he was puzzled. Then, when the ship was safely berthed, the maitre d' from the ship's hotel staff raised four fingers and the first four men in line came aboard. It was now clear. They were to be employees of the concessionaire who ran the ship's food and room service.

A few days later Brother Pedro talked with one of the four workers. Had he signed a contract? Brother Pedro asked. "No, not yet." Had he been told the terms of his contract, the number of hours he would work each day, the length of service? "No, I was just told to start at six." Did he know the rate of pay he would receive or his benefits? "No, I haven't been told, but I'm supposed to see the purser tomorrow."

The seafarer said he had been waiting in line every Thursday for almost a year, hoping for a job on the *Victoria*. He was so thrilled to be working on a luxury cruise ship after the long wait that he had not questioned anyone about the terms of his employment. He trusted they would be fair.

In fact, there were no contracts on the *Victoria*. Each seafarer signs his or her name in a registry book, along with a permanent address, his or her passport number, and the names of next of kin. The terms of employment are not available in writing.

What are the bargaining strengths of seafarers who are hired under such conditions? Can they be dismissed as quickly as they are hired? If the dismissal is unjustified, what procedure is there, if any, to redress their grievances? Can those in authority do anything they want to the crew, with impunity? This chapter examines these questions.

The situation of a twenty-eight-year-old Liberian seafarer who was being sexually harassed by a first assistant engineer highlights some of the injustices. The seafarer complained to the captain but to no avail, whereupon the seafarer asked to be transferred to another ship owned by the same company. When his request was denied, he asked to be repatriated. This request was granted at company expense. The seafarer's problems were not over, however. On signing off, he received an evaluation indicating that his work was unsatisfactory and recommending that he not be rehired. In his two years with the company he had never before been reproved for the quality of his work, and he was stunned to be unemployed through no fault of his own.

To whom could the seafarer appeal? The ultimate authority on a ship is the captain, but what if the captain is the problem? In some cases the captain may want to intervene when there is a problem but finds his authority jeopardized by others. The captain is the management's representative on board, and as such his freedom is often limited by shoreside decisions. In other cases, his authority may be compromised; he may be in the ambiguous position of knowing that the company has designated someone else on board, perhaps a lesser officer, to observe his actions.

There is an endless variety of ways in which today's merchant seafarers, especially those from the Third World, are abused. Nonetheless, the offenses fall into several major categories: contract disputes, wage abuses, problems regarding termination, issues having to do with health and living conditions, employment in a war zone, relationship problems, and reprisals.

On marginal ships, management is often guilty of a combination of offenses; if the crew's conditions are unsatisfactory, there are likely to be safety violations as well. Ports have inspectors who check on safety violations. Sometimes they are called in as part of an effort to delay a sailing and give advocates for the seafarers time to pursue other problems. If more time is needed, the U.S. Coast Guard or, if the ship is in Europe, Memorandum of Understanding for Port State Control inspectors will sometimes be called in to inspect for safety violations, further delaying the sailing.

According to traditional maritime practice, seafarers are supposed to be provided with articles of agreement, detailing the terms of employment.[1] Ancient maritime law describes articles of agreement to which the seafarer signed his name or made his mark. The basic contents of today's articles are included in International Labor Organization Convention No. 22 of 1928, now ratified by fifty-two nations.

In addition to providing information about the seafarer, the articles are supposed to specify the seafarer's job on board; the wages to be paid, both base and overtime; the number of days of paid vacation and holidays; and when the job is to be terminated. Furthermore, the laws of various maritime nations stipulate that whoever signs these articles must understand what he or she is signing. Management is supposed to give each seafarer a copy of his or her articles or post a copy on board the ship where it can be seen.

There is a great deal of confusion concerning the difference between a seafarer's employment contract and the articles. Usually a seafarer and his recruiter, acting as an agent of the ship's operator, sign the contract in the seafarer's home country. The seafarer and the captain, acting on behalf of the shipping company, sign the articles of agreement on board the ship.[2] The legal status of the contract signed in the recruiter's office is ambiguous. The laws of the registering country treat the articles as the binding contract. But if details in the articles—wages, working hours, and other terms—are not as good as they were in the original contract, there is not much that can be done. Once the seafarer is aboard the vessel, he must accept the wage and terms of employment dictated by the ship's operator.

Many seafarers report that they were never given either articles or a contract or that they were asked to sign blank contracts. Without a contract in writing, a seafarer is at the mercy of the ship's operator. Many seafarers have complained that they were promised terms of employment but have no proof of those terms.

Contract abuse begins in the recruiting office, where seafarers are often asked to sign blank contracts or bogus agreements. The following excerpt from a letter written by a Filipino seafarer makes this point, despite the broken English.

> *Due to the shrewdness of the manning agency who hired us in Manila just before we left we had three contracts made for us. And it was during the last few days before our flight, as if pinning us down, seeing us helpless with no time left to back off. Backing off then would put yourself at their mercy either to lose your job or be blacklisted. We really had no way to protect ourselves during those bogus meetings and orientation sessions. They call it a collective bargaining agreement, but it's only the management's agreement. I think it is quite clear then for you to understand our fear. They can easily outmaneuver us and dupe us out of what is rightfully ours.*

Seafarers are often required to sign two sets of contracts, each describing different terms, so that the ship's operator can meet requirements established by various officials and international labor unions in ports of call. If any of the contracts represent the true terms of employment, it is surely the one that least benefits the seafarers. Some ships keep two totally different sets of accounts and insist that the seafarers participate in the fraud by signing monthly pay slips indicating that they received higher wages than they were actually given.

Members of the crew of a large bulk carrier, all ratings (non-officers) from the Philippines, signed blank contracts at their agent's office in Manila. The crew members were content with their wages until suddenly all of them received a 30 percent reduction in their base pay and none of them received overtime or bonus pay for dangerous work, which they had been receiving. Without the crew's knowledge, the ship's operator had changed its registry from West Germany to Cyprus and had arbitrarily changed the terms of the contract.

When asked if they wished to appeal their case to the Philippine authorities, the seventeen Filipino seafarers resisted, fearing for their jobs. They knew they had signed blank contracts that could be filled in with lower pay rates. Besides, what good was the contract when the country that would enforce it was no longer involved in the operation of the ship?

The number of cases in which contracts are ignored is staggering. Antonio Inancio Pereira, for example, joined a Greek ship as chief cook in July 1985, whereupon he signed a one-year contract. When the ship called at Piraeus, however, early in January 1986, the captain engaged a Greek cook and told Pereira he would have to leave the ship in two weeks when it reached Bhavnagar, India. What could he do? The contract he had signed was good for seven more months. Would the Cypriot authorities who had registered the ship force the captain to honor Pereira's contract? Would the Indian port authority get involved? Would the Greek shipowner come to his aid? Typically, the answer to all of these questions is no.

With two exceptions, all members of the crew must sign articles. The exceptions are cadets, who fulfill academic requirements by working on board, and so-called supernumeraries. Normally, supernumeraries are company representatives or other workers who are performing an unusual function on board, such as technical electronic repairs. Supernumeraries are not considered regular crew members and are therefore even less protected. Employing supernumeraries in the place of crew to perform standard maritime duties is outside traditional maritime practice.

Early in January 1986, the Center for Seafarers' Rights received the following letter:

> We are three Tanzanians, three Sri Lankans and three Indians on a Greek ship with an otherwise all Greek crew. Our contract papers are totally false—we have not signed articles, and we are not listed in the crew's logbook. Technically we are told we are not members of the crew, but we must work all the time and receive only $170 a month.

The author of this letter eventually recovered considerable back pay and was repatriated. I do not know whether the others received additional compensation.

Bilateral agreements are another recurring contract problem. Nothing is more demoralizing than to be working side by side on a ship with a co-worker who is doing the same work but receiving twice as much pay. The United Nations' Universal Declaration of Human Rights, which has been the accepted international standard of human justice since 1948, states clearly in Article 7(a) that all workers have a right to equal pay for equal work. Unequal pay for equal work has become a maritime commonplace, however, especially on Greek ships. In January 1983, the Greek government passed a law allowing the Union of Greek Shipowners to pay foreign seafarers according to a scale it negotiated with the maritime unions involved. The Greeks on board would be paid according to the Greek union scale. Eager to find seafaring jobs, some Third World unions agreed to very low rates of pay.

The constitutionality of bilateral agreements was challenged in the Greek courts by the Greek unions. Several years of arguments and appeals followed, but eventually the Supreme Court agreed with the shipowners that non-Greek nationals on Greek ships could be paid less than Greeks doing the same work.[3]

In some cases, the owners of Greek ships simply pay lower wages even though there is no agreement with a Third World union. And in other cases in which there is no Third World union, a recruiting agent simply works out a deal with the shipowner.

Other wage inequities are also common. In a 1983 master's thesis on seafarers' problems aboard ship, Captain Colin Smith calculated that out of 165 cases he surveyed, 49 percent involved problems with wages.[4] The Center for Seafarers' Rights has calculated that 30 percent of its 1,600 cases involve wage claims.

Basic wages among seafarers vary tremendously from country to country and ship to ship, ranging from a high of more than a thousand dollars a month for Norwegian or American able-bodied seafarers on a ship from their own country to fifty dollars or less for seafarers from the People's Republic of China who are working on flag-of-convenience ships. Once the shipowner and the seafarer have agreed on a rate of pay, the seafarer has a fundamental right to receive the agreed amount.

The author of the following letter was a Kenyan who worked on an Italian-owned, Panamanian-registered vessel that sailed exclusively between Indian Ocean ports. He included a copy of his contract, duly signed by him and the ship's captain.

> I've come to this writing because I couldn't stand no more to our ordeal aboard the Sarah C. I've worked willingly due to my financial needs. But it's too much now. We could not stand no more. Too much work including every day Saturday and Sunday. No rest and some months no pay at all. Please help us.

According to the terms of his contract, the seafarer was supposed to receive eighty dollars a month for a regular 48-

hour week. He was also required to work 124 hours of overtime each month, for which he was to receive a fixed sum of thirty dollars. According to his contract, "It is understood that when not performed, the amount shall be reduced proportionately."[5] There was also a provision for vacation pay. If the seafarer worked continuously for 365 days without a day off, he would be paid six days' vacation pay or $17.75. In other words, the sailor worked seventy-six hours a week. For the first forty-eight hours of work, he received $.37 an hour; for the twenty-eight hours of overtime each week, he received $.24 an hour. One week's wages was $24.48, or an average of $.32 an hour.

A sad case, which eventually went to a high court in Kenya, involved Kenyan seafarers on a Panamanian freighter who were trying to get restitution for money they had not been paid. They assumed they were entitled to a minimum wage, even though they had no contract, and pleaded with the government of Panama for an affidavit stating the legal national minimum wage that applied to seafarers on Panamanian ships. Unfortunately, their pleas went unanswered; the seafarers lost their case and received no pay.

In a subsequent case in New Orleans, an expert from the Panamanian Ministry of Labor testified that the minimum salary in Panama was $.59 an hour. That information was not sent to the Kenyan seafarers, however.

Seafarers quite naturally assume they are protected by some system of law and justice. Only when they make a claim do they realize that they are in effect in a legal black hole while they are at sea. They are at the mercy of the ship's operator.

Shipowners and operators try to justify the low wages paid to seafarers by saying the workers make more than they would at home. But just because a worker can make only starvation wages at home is not a justification for a ship operator from an industrialized country to pay starvation wages at sea. A tube of toothpaste costs a dollar in Mombasa, Kenya, for example, the equivalent for a Kenyan seafarer of three hours' wages. Many standard food items are equally expensive. Yet seafarers throughout the world are expected to support themselves and their families on $3.50 a day. Employers as well as managers and registering countries— the "indirect employers"—are contributing to this gross injustice.

In fulfillment of the terms of Convention No. 109, the Minimum Wages Convention, the International Labor Organization has established a worldwide minimum salary, which in 1991 was set at $286 a month for able-bodied seafarers and engine room oilers. Only ten countries have ratified the convention, however. According to ILO procedures, a minimum number of countries have to ratify a convention for it to become law. In the case of Convention No. 109, this minimum has not been reached. Thus the ILO can only suggest that seafarers receive a minimum of $286 a month; it cannot make it a requirement.

The Philippine Overseas Employment Administration has agreed to use the $286 figure as a guideline and theoretically will not approve a contract if the stipulated wage is any lower, but there are obvious ways around this rule. A December 1987 report by the POEA indicated that of 4,612 ships surveyed, 776 paid exactly the minimum, which was $276 at the time, 430 paid less, and 3,406 paid more. One would be hardpressed, however, to find a port chaplain who has not heard seafarers lament, "We are not being paid our full wages. We are already months behind."

Sometimes a captain will do his best to secure proper wages for the crew but gets dismissed by the owner for doing so. The following report was written by the chaplain in Mombasa, Kenya.

> The captain and chief engineer came to see me in great distress with stories of underpayment, lack of payment and lack of payments to families for periods ranging from five to eight months. The majority of the crew had not been properly paid for one year—only local advances instead of payment in dollars as per their contract.
>
> They also claimed that the ship was unseaworthy and pro-

duced documents to prove it. I later visited the ship and there were indeed holes in the deck, cracked bulkheads and a hull that looked as if a sharp kick would have holed her.

They showed me copies of telex messages sent to the owner requesting payment, etc., also to the authorities in Limassol, Cyprus, where the ship is registered. As often happens in these cases there were both wage claims and safety violations. The captain hoped to use the safety issues to gain time to bring a wage claim.

I contacted the Port Authority, who told me they could not prevent the ship from sailing but that the agent could. I subsequently contacted Seaforth Shipping, the agents, and spoke to a Mr. Tom Miller, who seemed to resent my "interference" and said that nothing could be done.

As this was to be the last port before Karachi and the scrapping of the ship, the captain and chief engineer, with the agreement of all the crew, decided not to sail the ship because of its unseaworthy state.

I was then advised to contact a lawyer specializing in maritime law, who that night came to the Mission to meet with the captain and chief engineer. After hearing their story he considered that there was a good case for serving a writ to prevent the ship from sailing legally.

In the meantime the owner had begun to marshal his forces and began to retaliate by a telex to the captain, dismissing him and the chief engineer and ordering them ashore to await arrival of the owner's representative and a new captain from Piraeus and telling them that they would be paid in full. The captain telexed the owner to confirm that he would remain in command until his relief arrived. Whilst he was at the agent's office the port police tried to prevent the captain from returning to his ship. The agents had called the police in order to comply with the owner's wishes but a senior police officer explained to the agents that this was not possible.

Later they experienced difficulty in returning to the ship by boat and it was only after I took them to the landing stage that the boatmen agreed to take them. Pressure was being applied from all sides.

Days passed and everything was quiet. The captain naturally

became frustrated and worried because he realized that he could not hold the ship here forever and always his main concern was for justice and fairness for his officers and crew.

We contacted the lawyer, who made excuses for the delay in serving the papers required. This, of course, gave the owner more time to act.

On December 23 I received a letter from the lawyer saying that he was no longer representing the captain and the chief engineer. I had previously tried to dissuade him from this in a telephone call. His withdrawal seemed puzzling.

On Christmas Eve a new captain arrived from Greece to take the ship on to Karachi. The previous captain and the chief engineer were taken by force from their ship by armed police, put into a hotel and later flown home. The chief engineer was able to call and see me before they flew. He felt that they had lost everything.

On Boxing Day two Filipino seamen, whom I recognized, turned up at the Mission in a distressed state. They had been taken from the ship before it sailed and put into a local hotel to find later that only a bed had been paid for, no food. They had also tried to get their due pay before leaving the ship but had been assured that the owner's representative, who was staying in the Castle Hotel, would pay them in full if they went to him. One man was owed $560 and the other $800 and at the time of their conversation with me they had been prevented from making contact with the owner's representative.

To date I have heard no more. I can only hope and pray that after so much trouble the owner will eventually pay that unfortunate crew in full. It has amazed me to see how much scheming can go on to avoid payment of what is rightfully due, especially when large sums are involved in cargo.

As far as I know the crew was never paid.

Sometimes a captain will go through the motions of paying the crew but subtract illegitimate deductions. Several seafarers on a ship flying the Cypriot flag were to receive salaries of $611 to $821 a month. After "deductions," they received between $120 and $180.

Various reasons are given for the deductions. Commonly,

money is falsely deducted for repatriation costs, for cash draws (advances), and for purchases at the canteen and the ship's store, commonly called the slop chest. I have also heard of seafarers who had deductions taken out for monthly "safety seminars" and "medical examinations" and for entertainment, including video rentals, although the crew members had never received anything for their money. In one case, seafarers were charged for an "Immigration Escort Service."

For years there was a dispute on ships flying the Greek flag over whether non-Greek seafarers should be required to contribute to the Greek pension fund (the NAT), as required of Greek seafarers. The argument was that since foreigners would not receive a pension from the fund, they should not be required to contribute. Nevertheless, in countless cases, a deduction was taken.

The Greek Supreme Court decided unanimously that such deductions were illegal, but some captains have continued the practice and foreign seafarers are often powerless to change the policy. A few complain to the Greek Coast Guard, which invariably succeeds in stopping the behavior, but only rarely do the seafarers get the money that was withheld. Hundreds of thousands of dollars have been withheld and never returned.

Seafarers are frequently paid a basic salary for the first forty-eight or fifty-six hours they work and a "fixed overtime," or "global overtime," regardless of how many or how few hours of overtime they work. In many cases this means that a seafarer is paid less per hour for overtime than for basic time. A letter from a seafarer on a Panamanian ship explains the situation:

> Before signing on we have signed a contract we haven't read, because we were rushed by our company, and since we all have experience from other companies with fixed overtime, we agreed to a contract of fixed overtime. But they didn't tell us that we have to work 120 hours [a month] in addition to our normal forty-eight working hours. We work daily four extra hours including Sunday.

At the time, the basic wage for a forty-eight-hour week was $276 a month, or approximately $1.33 an hour, whereas the rate for overtime was a fixed $83 a month, or $.69 an hour. The Panamanian law says overtime should be one and one-quarter times the regular pay. For 120 hours of overtime, the crew should have been getting $1.66 an hour, or $199 a month.

Problems often arise over whose records are credible—the officer's or the rating's—especially if the contract specifies that overtime is to be paid based on the actual number of hours worked. The following letter was from a seafarer who was terminated when he challenged the way his overtime hours were calculated.

> When I boarded the **Mando V** *on November 29 we were two wipers, but unfortunately my co-wiper met an accident and one of his fingers was cut off and he was sent home. Since then I alone was obliged to do the daily chores of two. When I listed my overtime, I was denied. Here is the work I did: refacing exhaust valve of main engine; chip and clean rust from inside fresh water tank; chip and clean paint around boiler when boiler was idle. All work done above was from January 1st to the 30th. I kept records of my hours—212—but the second engineer allowed only 52 hours. Since I know the chief engineer has the final say in this matter, I waited for him. But he remained silent and I was sent home. I have served this company for ten years. But now I have no job.*

According to Liberian maritime regulations, for example, a seafarer must be paid overtime after he has worked eight hours in any one day. But I know of a Honduran on a Liberian ship who discovered, after he signed a contract, that the words "forty-eight hours" had been whited out and the contract changed to read that he would be paid overtime after seventy hours.

Filipino workers have special problems because of Executive Order 857 (February 1, 1983), which requires that their employers send a percentage of the workers' wages to their recruiting agents in the Philippines, who are supposed to allot the money to a person designated by the worker. There can be considerable corruption at this point. The agency receives the money in the currency of developed nations—dollars, deutsch marks, or yen. It is supposed to be deposited in a local bank and then credited to the allotees' account in pesos, at the official exchange rate. No interest is paid to the worker, even though it sometimes takes as long as four months for the money to be credited to an account. Furthermore, redress procedures are slow and appear to be weighted on the side of the recruiting agency.

Under the terms of Executive Order 857 as amended, employers of Filipino seafarers are supposed to remit 80 percent of their wages to their recruiting agencies. Most seafarers complain not about having to send the money to the Philippines—most are working to send money home—but that the percentage is predetermined and that the money has to work its way through the bureaucracy of the agency and is not sent directly to their dependents.

It is not unusual for Filipino seafarers to discover that their dependents are not receiving the allotment. Most seafarers today have accepted the hardships of life at sea and the prolonged separation from family and community so that their families can be fed and clothed. What can the seafarers do? They may not even know who is cheating them—the shipowner by not paying the recruiting agent or the agent by not depositing the money in the allotees' account.

I have heard of cases in which captains left a ship with the crew's wages. More often, the seafarers wait and eventually receive a fraction of what they are owed.

The crew of the *Jhoffa* had always received its wages from the captain approximately every month. Normally, when the ship was in port an agent hired by the company came aboard and gave the wages to the captain, who distributed them in cash. The captain's contract was over in July 1989, however, when they were in Dar es Salaam, Tanzania, and he flew home to Poland before paying the crew for the previous month. The owners claimed they were not responsible because they had sent the money to the agent; the agent insisted he gave the money to the captain. Regardless of the truth, the seafarers never received the money to which they were entitled.

Stories of abandonment by the owner are more dramatic than stories of wage disputes and unfortunately are also common. The following account of an abandonment is from the Sydney, Australia, *Daily Commercial News* of May 2, 1986.

> *Ten Latin seamen will learn today whether they can escape the red tape that has trapped them penniless for five months on a rusty cement ship in the shadow of the Statue of Liberty. The plight of the crew of the* Court Carrier *underscores a growing problem in the maritime industry, owners abandoning vessels to escape debts. Today, the United States marshal will sell the 1,991-ton freighter and its 4,000 bags of cement at public auction. The ship had a fire at sea, and limping into port two weeks late, the buyer refused to accept the cargo. In debt, and with no buyer for the cement, its owner abandoned ship, cargo and crew. The brass plate owner of the ship, Courtney, Incorporated, with a Miami address, could no longer be found. "Moved. No forwarding address." Meanwhile the unpaid crew are in limbo. "No one is responsible for them," reported an insurance spokesman.*

Abandonment by the owner is so common that most chaplains, sooner or later, have to deal with the problem. Quite simply, some owners, hiding securely behind a corporate veil, walk away when their bills exceed the value of the vessel.

It sometimes takes the crew and others involved a while to realize what has happened. Crews are often very trusting of the shipowner. The crew may not have been paid for months, but that is common. The captain may not be receiving instructions from the owner, but he has had to wait before. The crew may not conclude that it has been abandoned until the owner's phone has been disconnected and there are no responses to telex messages and no further instructions. Sometimes the seafarers are still disbelieving, even after liens have been put on the ship by chandlers, fuel suppliers, stevedores, and others.

Finally, when there is a shortage of food and no more fuel for the generator, the crew has no choice but to hire legal counsel and take out a lien for back wages. The lawyer, appearing in federal court, seeks a lien against the ship on behalf of the crew. The court then hires a marshal to arrest the ship until the liens are satisfied by the shipowner. If the shipowner does not respond, then the court sells the ship at a public auction and uses the proceeds to satisfy the liens.

Once there is a lien on the ship, the seafarers' contracts cease to be valid. The seafarers usually can remain on the ship during the months they must wait for the case to be settled, but the obvious question arises as to who will pay for their food and other necessities. Eventually, the proceeds of the sale of the ship are divided among the lien holders. Legally, after court costs are met, the seafarers' claim for wages takes priority over other claims, but an abandoned ship is usually not worth very much, and only rarely do the seafarers recover all they are owed. Sometimes there is not even enough to pay the crew members for their tickets home. As a last resort, the country where the ship is registered will sometimes pay repatriation expenses. Most will not, leaving the seafarers at the mercy of the host port.

A crew that is abandoned in a strange land is a victim of abuse by the shipowner who has walked away but is also an easy prey for others who through ignorance or malice may increase the seafarers' misery. I know of several cases in which incompetent lawyers agreed to represent abandoned crews and made the situation worse. Captain Miguel Lipardo, who was abandoned on the *Tara*, sought restitution unsuccessfully for years, as the following letter describes:

> The auction sale of the vessel was made in order to meet our back wages, together with administrative expenses. Everybody has taken their share and the remaining crumbs have been allotted to us. The award has not bettered our conditions, but purveyed more insult and injury. It has not redressed the grievance. We waited, bided our time, stretched our dwindling patience, endured the empty stomach, trusting in the legacy of

the law, the sweet statements about democratic processes, always hoping to attain deliverance, yet only to be rewarded with mental distress and frustration.

Now where is the promise of justice? We sought, we asked, we implored, relying on its integrity and benevolence. Yet even our California lawyer, recommended by our Consulate, our very own kind, color and breed, has taken us for a ride right under the eyes of your powerful country which claims to be a bastion of human rights, the very advocate of rights upheld, defended and protected by the U.S. Constitution.

It is clear that our settlement, our case No. 83–0429, was not a triumph of justice, but a grave injustice from which we the seamen will long suffer.

It is my contention that a ship is not a prison and that if a seafarer wants to leave a vessel, he or she has a right to do so, in the same way that a shore-based worker can quit a job. There are obvious limitations on a ship, and securing a replacement may take time, but usually it is a matter of days.

There are many reasons seafarers might want to terminate their contracts prematurely. During civil disturbances in Burma in September 1988, for example, several Burmese crews requested repatriation. Communication was cut off, and they were worried about their families. Similarly, several Jamaican crew members wanted to go home after Hurricane Gilbert devastated their island and they were unable to contact their families. In both of these cases, the requests were granted.

In other cases, seafarers have been denied permission to go home, even in emergencies. A Polish seafarer had completed his contract on an orange juice tanker registered in Cyprus when he learned that his wife was gravely ill in Poland. He was desperate to go home, but the captain refused to let him. In the port of Wilmington, Delaware, the seafarer, who spoke no English, methodically went through the phone book, calling everyone with a Polish name, until he finally found someone who spoke Polish and put him in touch with the

Seamen's Church Institute of Philadelphia. The chaplain there exerted the necessary pressure and the man was repatriated. Generally, seafarers who terminate before the end of their contracts must pay to be repatriated. Sometimes, for humanitarian reasons, the ship's operators will pay in an emergency.

For two years I received regular correspondence from a South African seafarer who had been allowed to fly home from Brazil, for what he thought was a one month's leave, when his mother became ill. Six months later, although he had made radio contact with the ship on several occasions, the captain never offered him his job back and he had not recovered back wages for several months of work.

In other situations, seafarers are ready to go home but are essentially forced to work past the termination date on their contract because the captain is withholding their final paycheck. Once they leave the ship, their chance of recovering their money is almost nil. Thirteen Chilean crew members on a Panamanian ship finished their contract in June 1986. Still owed several months in back wages, they requested that they be paid and repatriated while the ship was in the United States, where the captain was required by law to pay the back wages. The captain insisted they stay on board until the ship returned to Chile. The seafarers knew from past experience that it would be very difficult to recover back wages in Chile and that they would have to continue to remain on board against their will. Fortunately, a chaplain in the United States was able to convince the captain to pay them and let them go.

Still other seafarers are dismissed prematurely without cause. A seafarer from Montreal with fifteen years' experience as a physician on cruise ships was told one evening that his replacement would arrive the next morning and that he would be signed off. The doctor objected—his contract ran for seven more months—but he received no explanation. He was simply removed and sent home without any indemnification for his broken contract.

A situation in Port Newark, New Jersey, in February 1987 came out somewhat differently, thanks to intervention by a chaplain. Four Ghanian seafarers on a Cypriot ship were told that they were being replaced even though their contracts did not expire for six months and they had excellent work records. They were offered one month's severance pay, which was considerably less than their contract specified. They adamantly refused and threatened to strike; they very much wanted to keep their jobs.

Meanwhile, port police had heard from the captain of the ship that the "Ghanian Four" were making trouble and that the captain wanted them removed from the ship and repatriated at once. Fortunately, the police phoned the port chaplain, who told the real story. Together they went to the ship. With four police standing over him, the captain quickly agreed to pay the amount of severance pay specified in the seafarers' contract, which was more than three times what the seafarers had been offered. The chaplain convinced the seafarers that this was the best they could do, and they accepted the terms. Money in hand, they left for the airport that night.

Termination is sometimes totally unjustified, as in a case involving a pump operator on a Liberian tanker. While the crew was discharging gas, shore personnel signaled that the shore installation could accept no more gas for the time being and pumping should be stopped. The duty officer (the second mate) sought instructions from the chief officer, but he was asleep and could not be awakened, so on his own authority the duty officer ordered the pump operator to shut down the pumps, which he did.

When the chief officer awoke and saw what had been done without his authority, he became enraged, began shouting at the pump operator, and, according to several witnesses, beat him. In an effort to defend himself, the pump operator struck the chief.

Later that day the pump operator was dismissed; he would receive overdue back wages from the recruiting agent, he was told, less the costs of his repatriation. The pump operator objected to this arrangement, but, threatened by arrest, he capitulated and was repatriated early the next morning. A chaplain attempted to intervene but was unsuccessful. The recruiting agent denied knowledge of the unpaid wages. There was no redress.

Traditional maritime practice requires that a seafarer be repatriated at the end of his or her contract at the operator's expense. Besides transportation, repatriation costs normally include food and living accommodations until the seafarer arrives at the port where he or she signed on, a port in his or her own country, or another port agreed upon by the seafarer and the captain.

Although most maritime labor laws require that the operator pay repatriation costs, the law is often neglected. Some cruise ships, for example, require that all workers pay for their repatriation in advance as a condition of employment. If the seafarer has not deposited the costs of repatriation with the company before being employed, money is deducted from his or her wages, as much as 25 percent each month, until the full cost has been withheld. Once this questionable practice became known, the ILO included a prohibition against it in Convention No. 166 (1987), which has yet to be ratified. Liberia has declared it illegal to charge seafarers in advance for their repatriation. The practice continues, however, on ships registered in other countries.

Quite commonly, a seafarer is dismissed "for cause," which then negates the operator's obligation to repatriate. Captain Colin Smith reports that it is not unusual at the "end of a contract for officers to provoke trouble to avoid repatriation costs."[6]

On cruise ships, supervisors often tell seafarers who complain, "If you don't like it here, you can go home." Since the seafarers have already paid for their return trip, the threat is real and the seafarers know it will be carried out at their expense. Should the supervisor tire of the seafarers, the removal procedure is simple. All the supervisor has to do is notify the Immigration and Naturalization Service in U.S. ports that there are undocumented aliens on board who need to be removed from the ship and the country. The seafarers often have no opportunity to appeal, no legal recourse. The supervisor can fabricate charges of incompetence or insubordination, and who on board will question his or her decision?

The threat of being abruptly terminated hangs over the heads of seafarers like a storm cloud. The uncertainty of finding another job, the fear that a supervisor will write up a negative report, the disgrace of coming home early, and the total lack of an appeal procedure are constant sources of anxiety and concern. In the isolated society on board ship, where procedures are fundamentally controlled by those in authority, it is virtually impossible for seafarers to avoid being the victims of arbitrary or whimsical decisions based on emotions, prejudice, or just plain meanness. Under many conditions, seafarers prefer to suffer great injustice rather than risk being terminated prematurely.

Health care is another source of concern for many seafarers who remain employed. Before getting a job, seafarers should receive a health examination to determine that they are "fit for duty." If they become sick or injured while they are under articles, responsibility for their maintenance and cure belongs to the company operating the ship. They are supposed to receive the best possible care at sea and then treatment on shore, at the ship's expense, if necessary. Sick or injured seafarers are entitled to full wages while they are being treated at sea and a proportion of their wages, along with room and board, for a certain specified period of time while they are recovering on shore. As long as an injury was not the result of deliberate misconduct by the seafarer, it does not have to be job-related to be the responsibility of the ship.

In spite of the tradition of providing for maintenance and cure, ships often attempt to avoid their responsibilities, usually by sending seafarers home as soon as possible after the onset of an illness or following an accident. A Colombian seafarer had been working on a cruise ship registered in Liberia for eighteen months when he began to complain of a sharp pain in his abdomen. He visited the ship's doctor three times but after cursory examinations was told that the pain was nothing. Still in pain, the seafarer saw a doctor in Bermuda, who made a tentative diagnosis and recommended tests at a hospital. The seafarer had the tests done while the ship was in New York and submitted the bills to the operator of the ship, who told the seafarer that the costs would be deducted from his pay. The ship's operator also said that, because of the seafarer's illness, he planned to repatriate him to Colombia.

The Seamen's Church Institute interceded on the seafarer's behalf while he was in New York, and after much haggling and attempts to repatriate the man, the cruise company finally accepted full responsibility for his medical expenses. As it happened, he was suffering from kidney stones and needed an operation immediately. The cruise company paid the bill, as well as the man's room and board during the period of recuperation.

Under the terms of the Jones Act, a seafarer of any nationality may sue in U.S. federal court if he or she is injured in U.S. waters because of negligence on the part of the owner of the ship on which he or she is working.[7] Sometimes substantial awards are made to seafarers to compensate them for their injuries and the loss of work that results. In many cases, the ship's operator tries to hustle the seafarer out of the country before he or she has an opportunity to retain a lawyer. And, sadly, in some cases, the seafarer may be sent to a shoreside doctor who is in collusion with the shipping company.

There is a doctor in New York, for example, who will apparently say whatever the shipping company wants, regardless of the seafarer's condition. I first learned of this doctor when I received an urgent phone call from a seafarer who had been sent to him. When the seafarer returned from his visit, the chief officer told him to pack up his belongings because the doctor "suspected he had throat cancer" and he was to be repatriated to Hong Kong the next day for further treatment.

A chaplain from the Seamen's Church Institute visited the ship several times in the next six days. After talking at some length with the crew, he learned that the chief officer wanted to get rid of the sick seafarer and was apparently conspiring with the doctor. The chaplain asked to see the medical report but was told that there was no report in writing. He then returned with the seafarer to the same doctor, who gave the man a cursory reexamination. The diagnosis was the same; the seafarer was "not fit for duty, but fit to travel." The seafarer and the chaplain decided to get a second opinion. This time they were told that the seafarer had only a minor ulcer that would quickly go away. The company had no choice but to keep the seafarer on board.

As of 1989 the New York doctor was apparently still working for the shipping companies. When a Greek ship came to Port Elizabeth, New Jersey, in March 1989, a chief officer, on advice from a chaplain at the Seamen's Church Institute, went to an independent doctor. The doctor phoned to say the officer had hepatitis A, that he was not fit to travel, and that he needed bed rest and liquids. The captain refused to sign him off and, ignoring the diagnosis, insisted that he go to the company doctor. The doctor treated him so badly that the seafarer refused a blood test. An ugly scene ensued that ended with the doctor and the patient scuffling in the doctor's office. The chaplain was unable to convince the captain that the seafarer was seriously ill. The ship sailed that night with the chief officer still on board, seriously ill and very contagious.

The record shows that some ship operators take little responsibility not only for the well-being of the workers entrusted to their care but, as the following letter points out, for the families after a death.

A sailor working with me died on board in Europe where the factory ship was processing fish. How much compensation was paid to the family? One hundred eighty dollars. Do you know what the company said? The dead worker is only a casual worker. How can one be a casual worker when he has worked every day for the same company for four years? Now what will his children do?

Another seafarer wrote about a co-worker:

He fell down in the water at 11 a.m. on January 17, 1986, while maneuvering the rope getting ready to come alongside. Only the second officer saw him fall. He threw the life ring to the victim. He was holding a walkie talkie and he told the captain that [the seafarer] fell into the water. But the German captain did not stop the vessel. He continued navigating to the discharging port. Fifteen or twenty minutes after the incident, the bridge called a patrol boat to pick up the victim, and the Coast Guard answered that they had already picked up the body floating on the water, not breathing anymore. The ambulance took him to the hospital but he was dead already. If you want to verify the case, you can see from the log book if they stopped the vessel.

Another case involved a radio officer who went down on February 17, 1974, with the *Seagull*, a nine thousand–ton Liberian ship. Since that tragedy his widow, Raina Junakovic, has worked ceaselessly for the improvement of safety conditions, through the Comitato Seagull, an organization she created for the purpose.

The *Seagull* was due in Genoa, Italy, from Casablanca, Morocco, on February 17, and since her husband always called as soon as he landed, Raina Junakovic was concerned when she had still not heard from him five days later. She called one of the ship's owners, who told her, "They must have run into a spot of bad weather; they must be sheltering somewhere or other." This frightened Mrs. Junakovic; a nine thousand–ton ship does not usually lie for five days in the Mediterranean without being noticed.

Embarking on her own private investigation, she learned

one week later that a search had not been initiated. Instead of easing her concerns, this information made her despair. She had recently sailed on the ship and had heard many tales from her husband and others about its safety violations. She had recently persuaded her husband to quit, and this was to be his last voyage. Unfortunately it was. By now a whole week had passed, and there had been no call to launch a search operation.

Two months later Raina Junakovic learned that an investigation is automatically initiated when there is a search operation. An investigation probably would have revealed the terrible condition of the ship, which almost surely would have meant that the owners' insurance would have been canceled.

Italian television did a special program on the *Seagull* in 1980. "As long as everything was hushed up," the narrator for the program noted, "the substandard conditions were covered up. The owners just waited for the strong current of the Sicilian Channel to carry all the evidence away."[8]

Out of the crew of twenty-nine on the *Seagull*, only one body was found. An autopsy showed that the cause of death was exposure, not drowning. Additional evidence suggested that if a rescue operation had been conducted immediately, some of the crew might have been saved.

For months Mrs. Junakovic investigated, seeking to ascribe responsibility for the disaster and to ensure that similar accidents would not happen. Eventually, in large part because of her efforts, the shipowners were prosecuted and jailed for negligent homicide.

Some months after the tragedy, Mrs. Junakovic and other family members of the victims of the *Seagull* were struck another blow. The Oceanus Insurance Company of Bermuda, which had insured the *Seagull*, sent all of them letters informing them that the company carried "no life insurance whatsoever on the crew."[9] There had been millions in insurance on the property but not a penny on the humans on board. It is the same in many accidents.

It has been a major goal of port chaplains to put a system in place to ensure that families are informed when a loved one is lost at sea, but in many cases the operator does not even bother to inform the next of kin. When a ship sank on Christmas week of 1988 off the coast of New Jersey, chaplains who knew the eight members of the crew whose lives were lost wanted to express their sympathy to the families. They discovered that not even the shipowner knew the home addresses of the members of the crew. The chaplains had no way of notifying the family members of the loss. The families learned about the tragedy months later, when there was no mail and no phone calls.

The sea holds its secrets, and there are times when disasters cannot be prevented and times when the circumstances of an accident are never known. Generally, investigations of accidents place blame on either the ship or the crew. Eighty percent of all maritime accidents are blamed on human error. The policy decision that has reduced staffing levels so low that seafarers must work sixteen-hour days in emergencies is never blamed in the accident reports.

Sometimes responsibility for safety violations can be ascribed. Rectifying the safety problems is another matter. "I was repeatedly breaking the law by taking the ship to sea; a normal situation," a captain has written. "Any positive inspection for safety or seaworthiness would have revealed hundreds of deficiencies making the ship unfit for sea. In practice, it is rare for any ship to be detained on such grounds. The laws are cosmetic."[10]

On April 17, 1985, a Greek ship, the *John P*, sank off the coast of Brazil. An oiler on the crew reported that there had been many safety problems during the previous voyages. Sailing from Argentina to Angola, for example, the ship had been loaded above the Plimsoll Line, the line painted on the hull that indicates whether the ship can safely carry the load. There were leaks in the covers of the hatch, and four hundred tons of maize cargo had been spoiled when sea water entered one of the cargo holds.

On the next voyage the *John P* had again been overloaded. Sea water had flooded the engine room, causing the engine to lose power and the ship to go aground. The ship got free and proceeded on its voyage, but sea water had gotten into the hull.

Two days later, the ship started sinking and the order was given to abandon ship. Only one of the two lifeboats could be lowered. The other was stuck and could not be freed. Furthermore, the crew had never had a lifeboat drill. The crew was rescued by an Iranian ship with British officers and taken to Buenos Aries, where everyone was apparently abandoned. Having received no pay for two months and having lost all their belongings, the seafarers did not know where to turn to get money for their repatriation. They tried to hire a Greek lawyer but to no avail. They then contacted a lawyer in Buenos Aires, who after some months was able to put a lien on another ship owned by the same company on behalf of the seafarers of the *John P*.

In the years since the ship sank, the crew members, who have returned to their home countries, have heard nothing more from the lawyer in Buenos Aires. They have concluded either that the case failed in Argentinian courts or that the lawyer was crooked.

Seafarers have a right to ship out with a certified officer, but, although placing unqualified officers is a crime, many get placed.[11] For an officer to be certified, he or she must have a minimum level of sea experience and pass tests given by the officials in the registering country. In many nations there is a comity arrangement wherein one nation will grant an officer a license if he or she holds one in another country. Occasionally, recruiting agents grant fraudulent certificates. Only rarely are they punished, however.

False licenses are also available for a price. The German journalist Christian Jungblut wrote a widely circulated article in the German magazine *Geo* in which he described how he was hired as a third mate. With no more than several years' experience sailing a fifteen-foot sailboat, Jungblut got German officials to grant him a document verifying that he had several years' experience as a skipper. He then took a three-day course on operating a radio telephone, for which he was granted a certificate of competence. A phone call to a Dutch shipowner secured him an offer of a job, in writing, as second mate on a freighter. With the offer and 300 Dutch guilders, Jungblut easily persuaded a Panamanian consul to issue him a first mate's license. Jungblut then set off for Piraeus, Greece, where a stay of a few weeks and a $450 bribe of a recruiting agent got him a job as a third mate on an 85,000-ton tanker, which he met in the Caribbean.

Departure from Curaçao was during Jungblut's watch. Having served only as a deck boy twenty years before and with no training in navigation, he was now in charge of navigating an eight hundred–foot ship made of 15,000 metric tons of steel and carrying 525,000 barrels of crude oil, as well as a crew of thirty-four men. It soon became obvious to the captain that Jungblut was incompetent, and the other officers had to cover for him. It was a risky undertaking, but Jungblut made his point.[12]

There are many stories of officers who were clearly unqualified. A seafarer who was hired to work as an able-bodied seafarer but who also held a license from Liberia as a third mate told me that once his captain called him to the bridge as they approached New York on a foggy night and said, "You've been to school. See if you can figure out where we are." None of the "licensed" officers on board had had radar training. It is not uncommon for a cargo ship to wait outside a harbor for another ship to lead because the officers know they are incompetent navigators.

During the investigation of the grounding of the *Pacific Charger* off Wellington, New Zealand, in 1982, it was discovered that several of the Taiwanese officers had fraudulent licenses. The captain had never had training in radar and had been given a class A oceangoing license without an examination, based solely on his experience sailing with a class B license. The first mate had had only one examination, and that was for third mate, and the second mate had obtained his license under dubious circumstances. They were found guilty of the loss of the vessel. Fortunately, no lives were lost.

The captain of the *Pacific Charger* was soon in command of another ship. That crew was not so lucky. The ship foundered, and all lives were lost, including the captain's.

Examples of abusive human relationships are also legion. The medieval codes of law suggest a more enlightened attitude toward human relations than prevails on some modern ships. Captain Colin Smith summarized the issue:

> *Some of these cases are very dramatic and shocking, involving as they do such incidents as the beating with a shot gun of an Indian crew member, being locked in a cabin by a master for refusing to enter a War Zone, demoralization, insults, racial slurs, physical abuse, harassment, threats of murder if the authorities are contacted, intimidations and imprisonment on board during smuggling operations.*[13]

The incident described in the following statement is not as atypical as one would hope.

> *My friend and I were in the cargo hold cleaning. At 9 a.m. the German chief mate, still drunk, showed up and attacked me—grabbed me by the clothes, shook me, and pushed me around—for what reason I do not know. I was shocked and surprised and scared because I knew I had done nothing wrong, and besides he's too big for me to defend myself against him and I was there to work and not to make trouble or to fight anybody.*
>
> *He reported the incident to the captain and reversed the story. The captain believed the mate and got mad at us without hearing our account of the situation. We were told to pack up and leave the ship within one hour. When we refused to disembark the ship and insisted that we wanted to work, the captain grabbed my colleague in the arm very tight and the chief mate pulled me by the hair and dragged me out of the cabin and pushed us off the ship as if we were animals. We tried to complain to the port authorities, but it was a*

wasted cause. Nobody helped us except the priest in the Stella
Maris [the Catholic Seamen's Center].

Or this from a third engineer on a Cypriot ship.

I was maltreated by the master. He demanded that I sign blank
papers which I refused to sign. He then physically assaulted
me, beat me, and threatened me to the extent that I genuinely
believed my life was in danger. Not only this, but he deprived
me of the amount of my wages, which he had calculated. When
I requested payment, I was forcibly handcuffed and removed
from the vessel in Piraeus and that way lost all my personal
belongings valued at $2,339.

One might wish, or even expect, that the violence Dana
described in *Two Years before the Mast* would be a thing of the
past. Mail to the Center for Seafarers' Rights provides evidence, however, that there is considerable violence today.

During this voyage Philippine crew were subjected to assaults
by the Japanese officers. (St. John's, Newfoundland, Canada)

One of the crew was attacked by the Chief Cook and cut with
a knife while the vessel was docked at Pier 6. (Brooklyn, New
York)

At the top of the gangway the drunk captain stood with pistol
in hand threatening the frightened seaman. (Houston, Texas)

The file is thick with such accounts.

Cruise ships present unique problems. A cruise ship is
staffed by large crews—between four hundred and eight
hundred people from as many as forty nations. The shipboard
experience of the passengers who spend a few days in this
artificial and glamorous atmosphere contrasts sharply with
that of the crew, who live in crowded accommodations and
work very long hours. Status depends not only on one's job
on board but often on the color of one's skin, national origin,
language ability, and appearance. Furthermore, many cruise
ships are fraught with interpersonal conflicts and intrigue.
Crew members carry on private businesses aboard, subcon-
tracting their work out to other crew. Others demand that

tips be shared. Waiters have to tip the cooks if they want their orders quickly. Crew must pay for good jobs and promotions, and uniforms do not get cleaned in the laundry unless the seafarer pays. I have heard several references to the existence of a "mafia" on board.

The problems for women can be especially acute.

> *Nick, the bar manager, turned out to be nothing but a constant source of trouble. On the second night aboard, he approached Barbara about going to bed with him. She tactfully declined his crude advances—Nick kept up his disgusting pursuit of Barbara. We had a rough time. He was a disgusting creep who just wouldn't leave us alone, and he was our boss.*
>
> *When I left that ship I finally had a phone conversation with the owner. He only laughed at me and said I was wasting his time. . . .*
>
> *I was very lucky that I had the money to get myself out of that rotten situation; but there are many who are not as fortunate. They have to stay and make the best of it because they have families to support and that is the weakness which this disreputable cruise line exploits.*

It is difficult in an international industry to establish objective criteria by which to judge living conditions. Inspectors whose job it is to evaluate accommodations, food, sanitation, and other matters under the provisions of ILO Minimum Standards Convention No. 147 have been trying to develop guidelines. Admittedly, many situations are a matter of personal preference or upbringing. Crew members from one country may complain that the food on board is inadequate because it is so different from their diet at home, yet a crew from another country may find it acceptable. As the following letter illustrates, however, as in every other aspect of a seafarer's life, he or she is powerless even in the face of injustice.

> *On November 20, eight Filipino seamen . . . came to the Felixstowe, England, Seafarers' Center. Their complaint was the amount of food they were getting. You know that it is difficult for them to complain on board for fear of losing their job. They tried to complain to the captain but there was no response.*

They claim that for breakfast they get rice, with an egg; for lunch, soup with rice, and for supper, rice with sometimes a spoon of fish, hardly ever any meat, fruit or vegetables. The manning agent which hired them told them that the ship was paying $7.00 per day per crew for food. And some crew members have been on another ship of the same company and they are getting more and better food. They feel the captain is responsible. He tells the cook every day what he can prepare for food. I think he is putting the money in his own pocket.

Colin Smith recounts an episode in which a British captain found eleven major deficiencies in the accommodations on the ship to which he was assigned in Hong Kong. The ship had no refrigeration; a serious infestation of rats, bugs, and cockroaches; no running water in the bathrooms; smashed wash basin drain pipes; choked bathroom scuppers; no lights in the cabin; no electric fans; blocked toilet bowls; broken ladders; accommodations littered with rubbish and soiled linen; and mosquito screens in place of doors, which had been ripped away. There were also many safety violations. The captain refused to take the ship to sea and returned home at his own expense.[14]

Failure to respect the dignity of human life results in a discouraged and demoralized work force. A Nigerian seafarer summarized his feelings.

As a young man I was proud and had a big hope for the future. But I am discouraged now. They work me so hard and the money I send home is not worth the misery of life on this ship. What can I do? My strength is gone. I have become a machine. . . . If I die who will care for my three sons?

Another problem merchant seafarers encounter may be less obvious: their status in waters in which a war is being waged. Merchant mariners are not military personnel; they are engaged in commercial transportation. The strict discipline and hierarchy among officers make life at sea sound similar to life in the military, although crew members are civilian workers. Occasionally, however, they are unwittingly drawn into military conflict.

During the Iran-Iraq War of the 1980s hundreds of seafarers—two hundred from the Philippines alone—lost their lives. Most were on tankers transporting oil from Persian Gulf countries.

What legal protections guarantee merchant seafarers the right to innocent passage? Can a nation arbitrarily exclude or attack ships in areas that it claims for its own? Since World War II, the United Nations has attempted to address these questions. Article II of the 1958 Geneva Convention on the High Seas says that the high seas are open to all nations and lists four basic rights to which all ships are entitled: freedom of navigation; freedom to fish; freedom to lay submarine cables and pipelines; and freedom to fly over the high seas.

The law is clear. Ships have a right to safe passage on the high seas and through territorial waters as long as the passage is neutral and innocent. But enforcing the law, especially when countries are at war, can be very difficult.

When cannons could shoot up to three miles, coastline countries claimed a strip three miles wide as their own. As the cannons got bigger, many nations extended their territorial claim to twelve miles, which remains the international standard under the U.N. Convention on the Law of the Sea, 1982. A nation can claim a two hundred–mile effective economic zone (EEZ) in which it controls the ocean's resources but not navigation. The Convention on Law of the Sea underlined that "the high seas shall be reserved for peaceful purposes"; "no state may subject any part of the high seas to its sovereignty"; and "every state, whether coastal or land locked, has the right to sail ships flying its flag on the high seas" (articles 88, 89, and 90).

During the Iran-Iraq War, many seafarers asked to be repatriated, at their own expense, when they learned that their ship would be entering the war zone. In several cases their requests were denied. In one bizarre case, the shipowner called the seafarers into the captain's office and held a mock "trial" in which he charged them with refusing to sail into the gulf. They were not allowed to speak in their own defense and were all terminated and repatriated at their own expense.

Earlier I discussed seafarers' fear of being prematurely terminated. Many suffer further once they are home. In August 1982, for example, a merchant ship flying the Greek flag sailed into Antwerp harbor. The fourteen Filipino seafarers on board had not been paid for months and were owed a total of $188,074.48 in back wages under the terms of the collective agreement that covered the vessel. In accordance with standard maritime practice, the seafarers brought their complaint in the courts of Belgium and eventually were awarded $100,000. They were satisfied. In the presence of Belgian and Greek authorities, it was agreed that they would be repatriated to the Philippines without prejudice.

When they arrived in Manila on September 9, 1982, however, the seafarers were arrested and charged with economic sabotage and robbery/extortion. Filipino authorities claimed that by taking their case to court, the Filipino seafarers had damaged the reputation of seafarers throughout the Philippines and jeopardized their chances of securing jobs in the future.

In the course of predeparture briefings Filipino seafarers are often required to sign an undertaking saying that any monies they receive over and above their contracted wages will be held in trust and returned to the operator when the ship clears port. At the beginning of this century this was known as a yellow dog contract in U.S. labor practice. According to the undertaking, if a union came on board and successfully negotiated a better contract for the seafarers, resulting in higher wages, the seafarers who had signed the undertaking would be obliged to give the ship's operator any money over and above their original, agreed-upon wages.

Seafarers are also forced, some at gunpoint, to return money they received as a result of legal action they initiated in port. In March 1985, Chilean seafarers on a Panamanian ship hired a lawyer in an effort to recover overdue wages. The lawyer put a lien on their vessel and was able to recover their wages, but when the seafarers returned to Chile, police acting in cooperation with the recruiting agent forcibly took the money from them.

Another case also involved a Panamanian ship, this one en route to Rotterdam. While in Philadelphia, the first assistant engineer expressed outrage to the chaplain there that the ship had changed flags, there was now a new contract, and from now on twenty-five dollars would be deducted each month from everyone's paycheck and forwarded to the ship's manager in London.

A chaplain from the Norwegian Seamen's Mission talked with one seafarer at length. He was angry but afraid for his job and therefore did not want to proceed with a case. Others had lost their jobs for complaining. The chaplain volunteered to speak to the captain, but the seafarer begged the chaplain to drop the matter.

In February 1991, the Center for Seafarers' Rights heard from a lawyer in St. John's, Newfoundland, that eight members of a crew from the Philippines had asked him to represent them in a case against some officers who had physically assaulted them. His letter went on to explain the circumstances under which seafarers were pressured into withdrawing their case.

> After the action was started, the crewing agent sent their manager to St. John's to persuade the crew to abandon their action. He moved into the same hotel where the crew were housed and took a room immediately adjacent to them. In due course he convinced seven of the eight seamen to sign a release. Considerable pressure was placed on the crew members. Eventually, all but one succumbed and signed an affidavit of desistance.

Another incident involved a Honduran plumber on the *Emerald Seas*, a cruise ship that flew the Panamanian flag. He made the following statement during an interview with a reporter for *La Voz*, a Spanish-language Catholic newspaper published in Miami.

> *Most of us work as seamen in order to improve our futures. Our countries are poor and we have to find work somewhere else.*
>
> *All of us have a goal to reach, but not all of us have the same opportunity; some of the seamen have very bad situations with salaries of less than two hundred dollars a month and work up to sixteen hours a day. The seamen accept these conditions with the hope that one day they will find a better company and earn a little more money, but some end up being fired because of sickness or accident without any real possibility of claiming the promised insurance, even if they have it. The life on the ship has little in common with that portrayed in the TV movie "The Love Boat." Unlike the officers, the ordinary crew member has very little relationship with the passengers. They cannot circulate freely on the passenger decks. They cannot go to the bars and discotheques, and sometimes they cannot even talk with the passengers.*
>
> *One could say that at the top of the ship there is a life of relaxation and pleasure while at the bottom there is a different world which is one of loneliness, hard work and suffering. Even the food is always the same, with the daily menus not changed from week to week. The passengers change each week, but the seamen remain for the whole year. When they are in port, which is twice a week, they have no shore leave, except for those who work in the dining area, and even they are only allowed a few hours with nowhere to go.*[15]

Immediately after the article was published, the plumber was fired, without advance notice. He was removed from the ship by the usual method. U.S. Immigration and Naturalization officials came to the ship, drove him to the airport, and put him on a plane to Honduras, using money he had deposited with the company as a condition for getting his job.

Before leaving Miami he wrote a note to Father José Paz at Stella Maris.

They are firing me for the simple reason of what I said to the newspaper. The cruise operators think that I have damaged the reputation of the company and they made the drastic decision to fire me. Perhaps their decision in some way confirms my statement. I spoke the truth. I leave with my head high. It is not I who am acting unjustly.

By now the skeptical reader may be wondering, "Aren't there any well-run ships? You seem to be painting your picture with a very wide brush, condemning a whole industry for the excesses of a few operators." Yes, there are thousands of well-run ships where crews are treated fairly and relations are good. Worldwide, however, living and working conditions are increasingly substandard. Port chaplains are almost unanimous in their conclusion that the situation is deteriorating. A chaplain from England wrote, "Morale is low and human life on board ships is cheap." Safety is increasingly jeopardized, and, most of all, human values are neglected. Seafarers are being subjected to gross injustices in the name of competition. As we shall see, the unions that might represent them are virtually powerless and the laws that might protect them are difficult to enforce.

FOUR
Unions—East and West

WHENEVER I describe the working conditions of modern seafarers, especially those from developing countries, someone inevitably asks, "But what about the unions; don't they protect the rights of seafarers?" Worldwide, the maritime labor movement is precarious. As we shall see, for a complex combination of economic reasons, in very few nations are unions able to exert any real pressure on behalf of seafarers.

To do justice to the question of the effectiveness of unions, one must consider several closely related issues: the maritime industry's dependence on the Third World, especially parts of Asia, for the majority of seafarers; the difficulty of organizing seafarers into effective unions; and the status of the maritime union movement.

Seafarers from industrialized nations, eager to protect their jobs, and employers, eager for cheaper crews, have been at odds for centuries. It looks now as though Western seafarers have lost the struggle. The great maritime traditions recorded by Herman Melville and Joseph Conrad, as well as Jack London and Eugene O'Neill, are now most evident in Asia.

Whether the West will be able to attract job seekers to a life of merchant seafaring is a serious question.

Western ships have always had some Asians on board. Because of the nature of international trade, it has historically been as easy to hire mariners in the lands where the ship was trading as it was in the ship's homeland. As a result, American ships have often had more foreign seafarers than Americans.

In the early nineteenth century, when ships were still propelled by the wind, many American lads took one sea voyage and then returned to land, cured of their wanderlust. They were replaced by another restless lad or, more likely, by a foreigner. The challenge of the American frontier absorbed the American imagination far more than the fortunes to be gained on the seven seas. Thus, by mid-century, when clipper ships were racing from America to the Far East, "few Americans could be found in the fo'c'sles of these merchantmen on deep waters."[1] Chinese routinely comprised the majority of the crews on these glorious vessels.

Records from throughout the nineteenth century of seamen's bethels in American ports show that Asians, including Chinese, Filipinos, and Indians, were often members of the crews and that "foreigners" made up the majority of the seafarers. Father Benjamin Parker, the first chaplain of the Seamen's Church Institute of New York, recorded in his diary in 1843, "Only about one fifth of the sailors are American, the others are English, Dutch, Swedish, German, Danes, Scandinavians and some few Spanish, French and Portuguese."[2]

To protect national interests, Western countries passed laws and signed written agreements through the years requiring crews to be from the ship's home country. A U.S. law requiring two-thirds of all crews to be American was passed in 1817 but "was disregarded as soon as it became the shipowner's interest to do so." There were many ways to circumvent the law. "Captain Clark had a Chinese cook shipping as 'George Harrison of Charlestown, Mass.' "[3] The

1817 law was later repealed, but similar requirements have been written into American law several times since and are still in effect. Today, by law, all the officers and three-quarters of the ratings on American-flag ships must be American.

In Britain, the Navigation Act, dating from the reign of Henry VII (1485–1509), limited all trade to the British Isles to ships registered and owned in Britain and crewed by British sailors. The law was on the books until 1848, but, like the American law, there were ways to circumvent it.[4] The industry had to do no more than define as "British sailors" those who lived in the colonies. Later attempts to limit berths to British sailors also failed.

With the repeal of the Navigation Act, the number of seafarers from British colonies multiplied rapidly. By 1911, 25 percent of the 170,000 seafarers working on British steam vessels were lascars (Indians on British ships).[5] By the end of World War I, British ships were employing many seafarers from China, West Africa, Yemen, Somalia, and Zanzibar. By the early 1970s, 30 percent of all crew on British vessels were from these countries.

Authoritative figures on the number of Third World seafarers today are not available. Port chaplains visiting ships estimate that three-fourths of the seafarers are from developing nations, the vast majority from Asia. I have been told that there are 115,000 government-registered Filipinos, 41,000 Koreans, 20,000 Indians, and 20,000 Burmese and 19,000 Pakistanis employed in international trade. Statistics on Indonesia are hard to find. This vast country with seventeen thousand islands may have as many as 80,000 seafarers on international ships. Some of these figures do not include seafarers who have made private employment arrangements and are therefore not part of government registry programs.

A maritime educator in Hong Kong told me that Chinese maritime schools trained 1 million seafarers during the 1980s. Does the Chinese government now plan to place these men and women in large numbers on international ships, undercutting many jobs being held by other Asians? Chinese officials have assured chaplains' groups that they have no such plan, yet, inevitably, to overcome unemployment and accrue more foreign capital, increasing numbers of Chinese will be employed in international trade. The "marketing" of Chinese crews is a growing industry.

The structure of the Chinese economy is such that Chinese seafarers could completely undermine existing wage scales. Shipowners are being told that a Chinese crew can be hired for $7,000 per month, or $84,000 a year, less than one-tenth what it would cost to hire a Western crew. The Chinese able-bodied seafarer receives as little as $29 per month and a captain $95. Ship operators who make decisions solely on the basis of price will not be able to resist such deals.

Without question, there are many highly competent Asian seafarers who can operate modern, technically sophisticated ships. There are also many who were "trained" in maritime colleges and technical schools where they received only a superficial knowledge of seafaring jobs. So, while large numbers of seafarers are unemployed, managers are complaining that not enough seafarers know how to operate ships safely and efficiently. Officers complain that increasingly they must work with people who are untrained or undertrained. Responsibility for the operation of the ship is often in the hands of one or two experienced people because the rest of the crew so seriously lack experience and knowledge. One result of this change in the level of competence is that the one or two people with experience are under intolerable pressure.

Seafaring will remain a chosen occupation in Asia, and elsewhere, only as long as conditions at home are less tolerable than they are on board ships. Singapore presents an interesting contrast to the Philippines in this regard. In 1968, Singapore decided to become a flag-of-convenience registry, ostensibly to increase employment opportunities for unemployed seafarers. But even before the registry was established, the employment situation was improving, and by the mid–1970s the country enjoyed full employment. There was no longer the need to send seafarers abroad to bring in foreign currency and hence no longer the need to promote the employment of Singaporean nationals on its open registry fleet. With full employment at home and an ever-rising annual per capita income, the number of seafarers shipping out of Singapore has declined rapidly from a total of 6,802 (out of 9,187 registered) in 1972 to 2,274 (out of 5,297 registered) in 1984. Of the 2,274 who were employed, 1,872 worked in international trade.

The number of Korean seafarers has also declined significantly as wages have increased on shore. Between 1985 and 1989, the number of Koreans working on international ships dropped from 51,000 to 41,000. Other nationals can be employed much cheaper.

In Korea, the reduced value of the dollar has contributed to the lower wages earned by seafarers and has resulted in a real wage decrease of at least 10 percent. Between 1981 and 1987, seafarers' wages increased, on average, by 7.4 percent, whereas the income of workers on shore increased by 12.6 percent. An engineer on a train (a job somewhat equivalent in value to that of a seafarer) earns an average of $1,150 per month in Korea. A port worker with five years' experience averages $1,100 per month. The average seafarer's wage is $800.

To maintain an indigenous seafaring community capable of sustaining the rapid growth of international trade, Korea now faces the prospect of instituting an operating subsidy for its ships. The subsidy would enable shipowners to pay Korean seafarers wages competitive with those they could receive on shore.

It should now be clear that seafaring is increasingly becoming a career for people in poor nations. People do not want to go to sea if their living and working conditions will be worse than they are at home. As Asia develops economically it will be more and more difficult to attract seafarers. Only the poorest Asians, from the Indian subcontinent, the Philippines, the South Pacific, and possibly China, will be willing to tolerate the onerous conditions.[6]

In his book *Workers on the Waterfront*, Bruce Nelson describes the policy in the 1920s of "lowering wages and conditions by seeking to displace experienced, union-conscious seamen with the cheapest labor supply they could find."[7] Sadly, he could be describing the situation today.

Seafarers have protested over their working conditions for centuries. As early as 1768, British seafarers from dozens of ships struck their sails and demonstrated tumultuously. Hence the word *strike*.[8] And in April 1800, a Baltimore, Maryland, newspaper reported that "a large mob of sailors turned out for high wages and were parading the streets of Fell's Point."[9] More recently, in April 1981, 240 Honduran seafarers employed by the Carnival Cruise Line stopped working when they learned that two Honduran seafarers had been dismissed, apparently without cause. None of these "strikes" resulted in the establishment of a union, however.

Union organizing has rarely been easy, but of all working groups, seafarers are among the most difficult to organize. One of the biggest problems is that, in contrast to workers in factories, schools, or offices, many of whom are together every day at the workplace, seafarers are rarely together in one place. Rather, they are scattered around the globe in small, isolated groups. When organizers for the International Seamen's Union of America began a serious U.S. membership drive in the 1920s, they estimated that 60 percent of the potential members were at sea under contract and another 20 percent were working on harbor vessels in the coastwise trade. Only 20 percent were ashore, possibly available to participate in union activities.[10]

As in other industries, once they were confronted with the possibility of a union, managers, or in this case shipowners, often obstructed the seafarer's plans. A hundred years ago in England, for example, owners recruited trainloads of "black-legs" (nonunion seafarers), housed them in several old ships that were set aside for this purpose, offered them limited social benefits, and signed them on as needed to replace union seafarers. During the same time, no one in the United States was hired who did not have a "fink book," as the seafarers called it, which a shipowner would issue only after a seafarer turned in his union book.

Seafarers who protest, such as the Hondurans mentioned above, often face severe punishment. With the cooperation of the U.S. Immigration and Naturalization Service, the shipowner had the 240 Hondurans declared undocumented aliens. Because the National Labor Relations Act does not extend to seafarers on foreign ships, the seafarers were not protected by law, and all 240 were fired. The next day they were bussed under armed guard to the Miami airport, where they were flown home on a chartered plane.

The ambiguous legal status of seafarers under articles has limited their freedom to engage in union activities. Even today, seafarers live with the threat of being accused of mutiny, and it is not unusual for a crew involved in a justified industrial action to be accused of mutinous behavior.

As recently as 1937, the U.S. Supreme Court decided against seafarers accused of mutiny. In August of that year, after the *City of Fort Worth* was safely moored to a dock, the crew struck the ship because the employer refused to negotiate with the National Maritime Union. The employer promised to negotiate and the crew returned to work, but the seafarers were fired when they reached the next port. Subsequently, the National Labor Relations Board reinstated the crew, but the case went to court, where the employer, the Southern Steamship Company, argued that the seafarers were guilty of mutiny. The circuit court decided for the seafarers: "We think that there is no sound basis for depriving seamen of this right [to strike] when, as here, their vessel is moored to the dock in a safe domestic port."[11] The U.S. Supreme Court overturned the circuit court's decision, however, and found the seafarers guilty of mutiny, according to the terms of a 1790 statute.

The charge of mutiny has not been brought in a U.S. court recently. Seafarers who seek legal redress of their grievances and hire lawyers to defend them are now called deserters by the attorneys for the shipowners, but the threat of being charged with mutiny still hangs over them.

Many seafarers from the Third World are well aware of the benefits of unions and collective bargaining, and many seafarers throughout the world possess a high level of working-class consciousness. What they lack is a way to transform this consciousness into action without the threat of immediately losing their jobs and being permanently replaced. Many Third World seafarers are well educated, sometimes more formally than the officers from developed nations under whom they serve. Adul is a Bangladeshi seafarer who was a schoolteacher at home. Economic circumstances in Bangladesh forced him to find a job at sea to support his family. He is not permanently committed to his new career, and although he would be willing to risk his seafaring job to improve the situation for others, he does not think any industrial action he would initiate or in which he would participate would benefit him or other Bangladeshi seafarers.

Other seafarers have a deep desire to improve working conditions but feel that there are no viable options for doing so. "May I join the Center for Seafarers' Rights?" wrote one militant mariner. "We are only two Sri Lankans on our ship and the others here are afraid, but we want to be part of your union." Such letters arrive frequently from mariners eager to join an effective worker organization. In our response to these requests, we inform the seafarers that, although we seek to improve the conditions faced by seafarers, we are not a membership organization. We can support them in their desire for a better life as seafarers, but we do not participate in the hiring process or enter into collective bargaining. By no definition are we a union. Furthermore, only rarely have we recommended a union organization. The obstacles in the way of today's unions prevent them from achieving effective industrial action.

One of the main problems is that many organizations are unions in name only. They do not have the best interests of the workers at heart. They do not represent the interests of the workers in cases involving wages and working conditions. Nor do they attempt to give workers increased control over their workplace. Finally, in no way do workers in these organizations have a voice in the decision making of the union itself.

How effective can unions be when employers are free to locate anywhere in the world, including countries where governments are so desperate for industrial development that they will make almost any deal imaginable? Likewise, how effective can they be when employers can ignore local labor laws and hire and fire cheap workers without any repercussions? Workers are powerless in these situations.

The model of the union in industrialized nations may not be appropriate in the Third World. Cultural values in some labor-supplying countries prevent union organizing as we know it in the West. Workers are often deeply loyal to those in authority, despite the working conditions, and have a profound trust in the integrity of someone in power, making it easy for employers to take advantage of them. Loyalty to the recruiting agent or to the captain inhibits many workers from taking a stand.

In Philippine society, for example, which does not claim to offer equal opportunity to its members, people often attach themselves to a sponsor or "patron"—someone with power or influence—who can help them get into school, get a job, or otherwise advance. Not only does the person then remain tenaciously loyal to the patron, but he or she is obliged to repay the patron for favors received. The obligation, *utang na loob* in Tagalog, is not quantifiable. Some Filipino seafarers consider that working under deplorable conditions and earning substandard wages are part of the process of repaying an employer for the favor of a job.

Dependence on a patron can become a way of life. Captains, often appropriately called masters on merchant ships, are respected not necessarily because of their competence or integrity but because of their authority. Filipinos are known to yield their opinions and principles to those of a leader in order to maintain harmony. Giving in (*pakiksama*) is related to a fatalistic acceptance of one's inferior condition. Western-style unions, which often confront the authority of the shipowner, are an enigma in Philippine culture, where subservience is encouraged.

Confucian values are very influential in much of East Asia. In some Asian maritime colleges, Confucian teaching on human values is part of the curriculum for officers. The faculty believe that the authoritarian structure on board ship will not work unless it is tempered by a Confucian respect for human relationships.

Furthermore, in Asia familial loyalty far outweighs loyalty to any other social organization. Until recently, for instance, crewing in Hong Kong was a family affair. One member of the family, usually a boatswain, recruited the entire crew from family and neighbors. A union that claims to take precedence over familial loyalties will not succeed among some Asians.

Overcoming such obstacles to unified industrial action has proved to be very difficult. Shore-based workers facing similarly abysmal working conditions, particularly in the West, could have more easily exerted unified power in overcoming their oppression. In the maritime field, however, the circumstances have rarely been right for collective improvement.

Western maritime unions have been concerned about the Asianization of their work force for many years. The great hero of the American maritime labor movement, Andrew Furuseth, was adamant in his opposition to the "yellow peril." So was Havelock Wilson, the flamboyant founder of what has since become the National Seamen's Union in England. He threatened a complete boycott of any ship with a lascar or a "Chinaman" on board.[12]

Both Furuseth and Wilson were willing to extend membership in their unions to "foreigners," but that did not include Asians. Furuseth claimed that one of the purposes of his union was to replace Chinese and Japanese seafarers with American citizens and workers who were eligible for citizenship so as "to relieve ourselves of the degrading necessity of competing with an alien and inferior race."[13] Furuseth promoted U.S. legislation intended to bring about a single international wage rate so that owners would have no reason to turn to foreign labor.

In 1901, Wilson said, "I believe that a foreigner has equally as much right to live in the world as a Britisher. The only point is that I want that foreigner not to undersell my labor and I want him to be as competent to do the work as well as I would do it myself."[14] Wilson's union opened offices in Europe and New York for the purpose of recruiting foreign seafarers.

According to a U.S. law from 1915, commonly called the La Follette Seamen's Act in recognition of its sponsor, sea-farers of all nationalities were free to jump ship upon arrival in any U.S. port, without fear of recrimination for desertion. They could then be rehired at the going U.S. wage rate. Seafarers who had been employed abroad for low wages could leave their ships in Boston, for instance, and take another maritime job at the rate that was being paid there. Silas Blake Axtell, Furuseth's hyperbolic lawyer, claimed that wages for some foreign seafarers increased by three- to seventeen-fold almost overnight.[15] The hope was that foreign countries would cooperate with the scheme and that soon there would be one worldwide pay rate. For various reasons, including the refusal of other countries to cooperate, the system did not work, and in 1921, after the financial collapse of the maritime industry, the idea of a worldwide pay rate was totally abandoned, at least temporarily.

During World War II, employment conditions in the sea-faring industry improved significantly. They remained acceptable until the oil crises of 1973 and 1976, which led to such a depression in worldwide shipping that operators had to hire crews from the East to remain profitable. Survival meant other radical changes as well, including hiring far smaller crews. But in spite of these changes, many American and other Western maritime companies went bankrupt. In

1970, for example, there were nineteen shipping companies sailing under the U.S. flag; in 1990, there were eight, and only three—American President Lines, Lykes Brothers, and Sea-Land—owned more than seven ships.

The Asianization of the work force has left union members in despair and relatively powerless. Thousands of career seafarers have been made redundant as their jobs have been given to Asians, and those Western seafarers who do work have had to wait as long as a year between jobs.[16] Tony Lane summed up the situation in his book *Grey Dawn Breaking*: "Seafarers have responded to the sudden and calamitous decline of merchant shipping with a mood that oscillates between anger and disbelief."[17]

Many unemployed seafarers have attempted to stop the flow of jobs to the East by seeking legislative relief. Others have formed advocacy groups, such as the Selbsthilfsgruppe (self-help group) in Germany, because they felt totally abandoned by their government and industry and could find no way to hold on to their lifetime careers. Unions have blamed various scapegoats, including the Center for Seafarers' Rights, which has advocated for Third World seafarers. To date, however, none of these efforts have been effective.

One of the problems is that maritime unions have lost their zeal. To hold on to the few jobs that are left, they have had to settle for far less than they did in the past. They simply do not have a strong bargaining position; they know that if they press hard for either higher salaries or improved working conditions operators will "flag out," that is, register their ships abroad and hire foreign crews. While aging union members fight for dwindling pension benefits, the officers fight among themselves for power, for the gold cards and the limousines and the trips on the Concorde.

Lest the maritime tradition and expertise disappear completely, unions in some countries are agreeing to let ship operators hire crews from developing countries if the senior officers they hire are members of the union. The Norwegian Seamen's Association, for example, has negotiated a contract with the Associated Marine Officers and Seamen's Union of the Philippines that states that two jobs on every ship registered with the Norwegian International Ship Registry (NIS) will be filled by Norwegians or by officers who meet Norwegian minimum standards of certification and education. The other jobs are usually offered to Filipinos. Even this agreement is not holding. Some NIS ships have no Norwegians aboard.

Because of their tradition of excellence in leadership and navigation, some Western officers have found jobs on foreign ships, but often for wages much lower than they would have been before the change in hiring practices. Meanwhile, Western deckhands and engine room workers are almost extinct, and the great seafaring tradition of the West is but a memory. As Nelson notes in *Workers on the Waterfront*: "The remnants of this once vibrant subculture barely exist today beyond a few shrinking enclaves."[18]

Havelock Wilson and Andrew Furuseth recognized that unions have to be organized internationally to exercise power in the industry. Shipping is perhaps the most transnational of all modern industries and easily escapes the influence of national unions. Maritime workers, recognizing this fact of commerical life more than any other group of transport workers, gave impetus to the creation of the International Transport Workers' Federation in July 1896.[19]

Throughout much of the twentieth century, the ITF has been a respected advocate for seafarers' rights in the international arena. When the International Labor Organization began in 1919, it was the ITF, articulately representing seafarers' causes, that ensured the adoption of several important conventions and resolutions. These included the establishment of a minimum age for seafarers, shipwreck indemnity, protection from recruitment fees, and a requirement that young seafarers be given medical examinations. In 1924, conventions were passed prescribing what should be included in articles of agreement and protecting seafarers from paying repatriation costs. During this period, the ITF was respected throughout the maritime world as the advocate for the fair treatment of all mariners.

Before, during, and after World War II, many shipowners transferred their ships to flag-of-convenience registries for political and economic reasons. After the war it was generally acknowledged that many wartime ships had become substandard, especially the so-called liberty ships being sold and reregistered by their new owners in Panama. At that time (as now), Panama exerted few controls over conditions aboard. According to a report that is not generally sympathetic to the ITF, shipowners at that time cooperated with the organization in its campaign to improve conditions on foreign-flag vessels.[20] It was in their own self-interests to eliminate the competition offered by these cheap ships.

Cooperation, with the goal of improving flag-of-convenience shipping, peaked in 1958 when the ILO passed Resolution 108, which sought to discourage seafarers from crewing foreign-flag vessels without collective contracts or provisions comparable to European standards. The resolution had little effect in stopping companies from flagging out, however.

In the years following the war, the ITF also became particularly concerned about the increasing number of jobs that were going to non-Western seafarers and it shifted its focus from eliminating substandard conditions aboard ships to the problem of economic competition from workers of poor countries. The mandate from the most influential affiliates was to protect Western jobs. The Special Seafarers Section of the ITF, which was created soon after the war to organize seafarers on flag-of-convenience ships and to bargain for them, now sought to sign collective bargaining agreements that would raise the wage rates earned by seafarers from developing countries to a level comparable to those earned by Westerners. Wilson and Furuseth's goal of a worldwide maritime wage rate was again in view with the ultimate goal of discouraging shipowners from flagging out simply to save labor costs. The campaign was quite successful, especially in England, Scandinavia, New Zealand, and Australia, where dockers (longshoremen) and other maritime workers could legally engage in secondary boycotts and thereby prevent ships from sailing until they signed collective bargaining agreements.

When an ITF affiliate organizes a crew and the collective bargaining agreement is approved by the London office of the ITF, the ship is issued a blue card and can sail freely around the world without union interference. Flag-of-convenience ships that do not have blue cards can expect to be boycotted in some countries where unions are strong and secondary boycotts are legal.

In spite of its success, the flag-of-convenience campaign had fundamentally conflicting goals. Western unions expected the ITF to ensure that jobs would not be given to lower-paid Asian seafarers, while the Asian unions hoped to gain a competitive advantage by working for lower wages. Keeping these conflicting goals in balance while advancing the flag-of-convenience campaign was a difficult task.

The campaign seemed to be going well until the National Union of the Seafarers of India (NUSI), a well-organized maritime union, insisted on signing contracts in which the agreed-upon wages, while beneficial to Indian seafarers, were lower than those that were acceptable to the ITF. NUSI was temporarily suspended from the ITF, and subsequently the Asian affiliates formed their own association. Since then, NUSI has been reinstated, but the Asian ITF affiliates continue to meet occasionally without representation of the ITF secretariat.

Maritime unions in the West, especially in the United States, have increasingly blamed the ITF for its failure to prevent the loss of jobs for Westerners. Worker solidarity appears to have geographical limits. American affiliates have noisily threatened to withdraw if the ITF does not succeed in stopping the spread of "runaway" flags. Furthermore, the ITF's fight to eliminate flag-of-convenience registries has preempted cooperation with those registries in seeking to improve conditions.

The ITF continues to talk about a worldwide wage rate,

and seafarers take that at face value, often assuming that union affiliation with the ITF will ensure them this rate of pay. In negotiations with flag-of-convenience ships, however, unions often settle for far less. In 1988, for example, under their collective bargaining agreement, able-bodied seafarers who were members of the Sindicato Unico de Oficiales de las Marine Mercante Nacional-CPV, an ITF affiliate, and who were working for the Peruvian National Steamship Company, were paid a mere $.44 an hour, or about $3.50 a day, far below the ILO suggested minimum wage.

When the wages the seafarers are receiving are lower than the ITF minimum, the ITF, in an effort to reduce the attractiveness of flagging out, sometimes requires shipowners to pay the union the balance of what it would have cost to hire a Western crew. Such an agreement is called a Total Crew Cost Agreement. For example, Russian seafarers on a Soviet-owned ship flying the Cypriot flag receive $520 per month, although the shipowner pays $1,300 per crew member per month. The balance goes to a central fund to be dispersed according to the requirements of a new Eastern European ITF affiliate, the Independent Union of Water Transport Workers.

Affiliates complain that the ITF secretariat in London is a wealthy, entrenched bureaucracy that is unresponsive to their demands. Seafarers often complain as well:

> The ITF man came on board but he would not listen to us. He told us what he was going to do. He told us we would get higher wages. And then he went to the captain's cabin. There has only been trouble since then. . . . It was better before.

> I have written to the ITF for five years about our case, but I never get an answer. They told us in Finland that we would get our back wages, but we have been waiting. Can you help?

The ITF has not encouraged the organization of new, autonomous, locally organized unions in the Third World. Rather, it has discouraged their creation in an attempt to preserve its hegemony in the maritime labor movement.

Many shipowners are very angry at the ITF for what they consider to be the unreasonable methods it uses to force shipowners to sign up for blue cards. A primary point of contention is the money shipowners must pay into the Seafarers' International Welfare Assistance and Protection Fund. The ITF established this fund for Third World seafarers, who do not receive social security and retirement benefits. Shipowners who enter into an ITF agreement must contribute for every seafarer aboard. The money in the fund has grown far more rapidly than it has been dispersed; in 1990, the capital value in two separate funds was approximately $200 million.[21] While some of this money is available for welfare projects of benefit to seafarers, it is also given out in the form of grants to local ITF affiliates, with the effect of controlling them. Affiliates in financial straits because of shrinking memberships are constrained from biting the feeding hand. The very existence of the fund is a cause of great concern to shipowners.

Despite many failures, the ITF still supports seafarers in several ways. It maintains inspectors in many ports, especially in Europe and the United States, who routinely respond to the living and working needs of seafarers, regardless of their affiliation. It continues to represent the needs of seafarers in the ILO; in the International Maritime Organization, a United Nations department concerned primarily with standards of safety; and in other international forums.

As I mentioned earlier, many Third World unions are not representative worker organizations. Those that effectively help workers struggle against exploitation by shipowners and serve as the workers' mouthpiece in the struggle for social justice are worthy of the name. But those that fail to perform these functions, regardless of what they call themselves, are not unions in the sense that I am using the term.

There are some authentic maritime unions in the Third World—in India and Indonesia, for example—and seafarers in other countries have attempted to create them.[22] The Concerned Seamen of the Philippines (CSP) was born during the vibrant time when many occupational groups were organizing to protest the presidency of Ferdinand Marcos. The CSP was first seen on the streets of Manila demonstrating against the oppressive maritime policies of the Marcos dictatorship. Since the change of government, it has continued to recruit members, investigate the situation of Filipino seafarers, protest against particularly repressive measures, represent abused seafarers in the courts, and organize coastal vessels.

The CSP was conceived by Captain Rogelio Morales, a former superintendent of the federal maritime school, the Philippine Merchant Marine Academy. Its development was not easy. As is common in the history of truly democratic union movements, there were various internal splits and divisions. After affiliation with the International Transport Workers' Federation was denied, it affirmed its international perspective by affiliating with the Trade Union International of Transport and Fishery Workers (TUI-WFTU). With ten thousand dues-paying members, the CSP has addressed some of the thorniest issues affecting Filipino seafarers, for example, publicly opposing bareboat chartering.

Under the bareboat charter system, a vessel is temporarily registered in the Philippines, using a Filipino corporation as a front. An all-Filipino crew is then hired, and the vessel is chartered back to the original owner for a specified time. The owner then operates the ship with the assurance that there will be no ITF interference since it flies the national flag of the Philippines rather than a flag of convenience.

At the beginning of 1988, 461 vessels were flying the flag of the Philippines, and of these, 432 were under bareboat charter. A total of 105 of these were chartered by recruiting agencies, solely to reduce crew costs.[23] Only the "marriage of convenience" between the Associated Marine Officers and Sailors Union of the Philippines (AMOSUP) and the ITF prevents the ITF from condemning this practice, which clearly undermines the ITF campaign against open registries.

The experience of three Chilean seafarers illustrates how

"unions" often undercut the interests of their members. Attorney John Merriam worked closely with a Chilean maritime union on their case, which involved their efforts to be compensated for wages they had not received while working on the Greek ship the *Mninosyni*. Merriam's report included the following analysis:

> *The National Union of Chilean Seamen in Foreign Vessels is nothing more than a store-front operation of relatively recent origin. 19.6 percent of the base pay for Chilean sailors aboard Greek ships are earmarked for personal social security funds in Chile. At least in my case, [the company] did in fact send these funds to Chile. The funds reached the union, but were not deposited in the designated banks.*
>
> *The* modus operandi *of this Chilean union is to first threaten non-compliant sailors. If this does not work, there is an offer of compensation in any amount to prevent legal claims against Greek shipowners. It is considered worthwhile to pay any amount in individual cases to avoid upsetting the applecart in the overall scheme of selling Chilean labor to the Greeks.*
>
> *Part of the compensation is having Chilean sailors pay a good deal of money to become eligible to be sent out on Greek ships. (One sailor paid $200 directly to the union; another worked for six months in the union office without wages before he got his job; another served as a Greek-Spanish translator.) A small headpiece is paid to the union by the Greeks for each sailor shipped. Each Chilean sailor is required to post a sizable good behavior bond (in the cases of my clients—the mortgage of the houses of relatives). This ensures that no wage or treatment claims are brought during the voyage. My clients escaped this because they did not bring their claims until after they had completed their articles.*

AMOSUP not only claims to be a union but is one of the most influential maritime institutions in Manila. The organization maintains a deluxe national headquarters that includes a seafarers' club, a hospital, a retirement home, a food co-op, and a housing complex.

The marriage of convenience between the ITF and AMOSUP appears to benefit both organizations. The ITF can claim that it has a strong affiliate union in the Philippines that places many thousands of seafarers. For its part, AMO-SUP can issue ITF blue cards, assuring that the ship will not be interdicted by ITF representatives in other ports. Because interdiction can be very costly, it is worthwhile for shipowners to deal with AMOSUP. ITF affiliation is the primary reason for AMOSUP's strength. It is clear, however, that AMOSUP does not help the seafarers in their struggle against exploitation by shipowners. In practice, AMOSUP is more sympathetic to the owners, who have the jobs available, than to the workers. The seafarers are called members of the union only as long as they are employed. There is no long-term loyalty in either direction. Seafarers often complain to the Center for Seafarers' Rights about having to pay AMOSUP dues, some directly to an AMOSUP office in London, knowing that there will be no benefits.

I received the following letter from a chaplain in Louisiana:

> On September 16, 1982, two Filipinos, R. S. Marinos and Daniel Arnada, were dismissed by the captain of the BP Humber. He called them into his office and explained that he was sorry to lose them, they were both excellent workers, and he gave them recommendations indicating that their conduct and ability were very good. He explained that he was under company orders and that the dismissal was at the request of AMOSUP, which had recently negotiated a new collective bargaining agreement at lower rates with the company and wanted all those who were still working with the old, more expensive contracts removed from service. I wonder what kind of pay-off the union President received?

Seafarers throughout the world suffer because there is no effective association with bargaining power to confront shipowners. Workers take what they can get while resenting, often silently, the working world that victimizes rather than respects them. The Center for Seafarers' Rights hears frequently from seafarers that the union movement is no longer effective and has even become part of the problem. Corruption, for example, continues to be a significant problem in both the East and West.[24]

> *I am able seaman working in my national shipping line named Black Star Line, Ghana. I belong to the National Union of Seamen, affiliated to the Trade Union Congress Ghana. Since the establishment of this company Black Star Line in 1958, there is not any proper Agreement between the company and the Seamen. The company has been cheating the seamen in wages, rations, working clothes, allowances, seamen entitlement, etc. but our seamen union could not fight for us to overcome all these problems. This allows the company to cheat the seamen more and more. Also the trade unions have become political organizations exploiting the seamen. There is always conflict among the seamen on a question of employment because our ships were few and the seamen are many and jobless.*

FIVE

Maritime Law and the Protection of Seafarers

MOST modern maritime laws do not have international authority but are passed and enforced by individual sovereign nations. There are some international maritime laws, but only a limited international mechanism for enforcing them. Shipping is by definition transnational, or perhaps more appropriately extra-national or extra-territorial. National states are the custodians of maritime laws, although the industry operates outside their boundaries and therefore their control. The result is that in many cases there are no effective laws that protect the working mariner.

Before the development of modern national states, a common corpus of laws existed that was honored throughout the Western maritime world—in the Baltic Sea, in the Mediterranean Sea, and along the Atlantic Coast. Evolving from the Rhodian sea law of the third and fourth centuries B.C., this common maritime law was codified in various medieval port cities as the Laws of the Hansa Towns, the Laws of Amalfi, the Consulado del Mar (Barcelona), and the Laws of Oleron.

95

Whereas modern maritime law deals mostly with ships and cargo, these ancient laws concerned primarily the rights and duties of mariners themselves. They established guidelines concerning a ship's liability in the event a seafarer was sick or injured, the length of the contract, duties requiring extra compensation, indemnity in case of a shipwreck, even the settlement of disputes.

According to article 12 of the Laws of the Hansa Towns, for example, contradicting a captain was punishable by a fine, and the captain had the right to strike the mariner with his fist or open hand, once only. If the captain struck him more than one blow, the mariner could defend himself.[1]

What was codified as maritime law in one port could be used in the courts of all the other ports. Some rather curious practices are preserved in these laws, which if they were still in force might improve the situation on some of the ships I have described.

> The mariner is obliged to obey the master, and if the master is enraged at him the mariner should keep out of his sight or hide in the prow of the ship. If the master follows him, he should fly to some other place from him, and if he still follows him, then the mariner may stand upon his defense demanding witnesses how he was pursued by the master, for the master ought not to pass into the prow after him.[2]

To illustrate how the law works, or does not work, to the benefit of seafarers, I have created a composite character named Ruben who faces some of the problems typically confronting seafarers today. Ruben is a Filipino third engineer who works on a Saudi-owned bulk carrier called the *Serrasalmo* that flies the Panamanian flag. The ship is a tramp; it follows no particular route but picks up grain, coal, scrap iron, sugar, and other bulk items wherever management can find cargo. The ship is relatively old and has a crew of twenty-eight men.

Today's crews are likely to represent almost any combination of nationality, but for the purposes of this example, imagine that most of the officers are Korean and the crew is Filipino, a combination that is almost guaranteed to produce tensions. Obviously, the recruiting agent had no understanding of the dynamics between various Asian nationals.

Ruben's chief complaint is that he is being beaten regularly and severely by the Korean second engineer, Mr. Kim. There are many management companies involved in the operation of the *Serrasalmo*, and Ruben can find no agent or manager who seems the least bit concerned about his problem. He has already appealed unsuccessfully to the captain and to the chief engineer. Ruben's only recourse is legal action. But where and how?

Ruben's home country offers him no legal protection while he is at sea. Consular authorities in some nations have traditionally accepted responsibility for the welfare of their nationals when there are problems abroad, especially if worker, owner, and flag are of the same country, but consular officials are often reluctant to disturb diplomatic relations when several countries are involved.

Ruben's next hope is the authorities of the flag state, in this case, Panama. Courts have consistently ruled that the flag state has jurisdiction over the internal affairs of the ship according to the principle of "roving sovereignty." Thus, a ship registered in Panama is considered a little piece of the territory of Panama regardless of who owns the ship or who is on board.

In the United States the foundation case in this regard was *United States v. Holmes*. "It makes no difference whether the offender be a citizen of the United States or not. If [the offense] be committed on board of a foreign vessel by a citizen of the United States, or on board of a vessel of the United States by a foreigner, the offender is to be considered, *pro hac vice*, and in respect to this subject, as belonging to the nation under whose flag he sails."[3]

A British decision of 1868 reflects the same opinion: "A

British ship is for the purposes of this question, like a floating island . . . and the offender is as nameable to British law as if he had stood on the Isle of Wight and committed the crime."[4]

There are no enforceable international standards of operation for the internal affairs of the ship. International practice does not impose any particular responsibility on the ship's flag state. If the flag state fails to enforce its laws on its ships, then there is no higher authority that can require compliance. Another state may make a complaint to the flag state or to an international body that certain international standards are not being maintained, but this complaint has no legal power to change the enforcement procedures of the flag state. Without flag state enforcement, the ships' operators are free to take the law into their own hands.

Considering the lack of standards on ships, it is not surprising that the sea has been the workplace, sometimes the playground and even the asylum, for independent adventurers and buccaneers who engaged in behavior that would not have been tolerated ashore. The Center for Seafarers' Rights files include a description of a ship on which everyone aboard works without salary and without complaint and several of the crew have worked under these conditions for years. Apparently the entire crew consists of fugitives who have found asylum within the sovereignty of the ship.

The seas have been the locale for some of humanity's nastiest business—piracy, rum running, and slave trading. The people responsible for these ventures have fled to the oceans, which fall far outside the influence of the law of civilized, land-based people. The oceans are also a symbol of opportunity and freedom, lying beyond the confines of any one state and belonging to all peoples in common.

Today, as forty countries eagerly offer shipowners very favorable conditions if they will fly their flags, the significance of ship registration has virtually disappeared. I have talked with seafarers who did not know the registry of the ship on which they were workers. One Indonesian said to me, "The name on the stern is Valletta; where is that?" The man was theoretically employed by a company in Malta and protected by the laws and courts of the Commonwealth of Malta, yet he was totally unaware of this.

In effect, the internal management of the ship is no longer controlled by a sovereign state but by a sovereign shipowner. The registering country has defaulted its responsibility to its workers by yielding all authority to the shipowners. The democratic principle of differentiation of power is lost. Whoever legislates also enforces and judges, leaving the citizens totally disenfranchised.

Most governments are highly influenced by the marketplace in the laws they enact and enforce and in those they neglect. When the sovereign nation of Vanuatu, for example, announced that it was establishing a ship's registry, the message was clear—it had no intention of interfering with the operation of the ship. Operators could behave as they wished and shipowners could hire and fire with impunity. Since it was established, Vanuatu, a tiny republic of only one hundred thousand people, has registered four hundred ships, although it has almost no consulates and no facilities for aiding its workers abroad.

The absurdity of the registry situation was illustrated when Sealand announced that it had registered a ship called the *Sarah*. Sealand is a tiny principality located seven miles off the British coast that is no more than a floating platform slightly larger than a basketball court. The platform is owned by a brash and eccentric British businessman who claimed his platform as a sovereign territory in 1968 and "declared himself as prince, his wife as princess, and proceeded to create a flag, a constitution, stamps and currency."[5]

As for Ruben, there is little likelihood that he would get much help from the country where his ship is registered, Panama. He could file a complaint with the Directorate of Consular and Maritime Affairs of the Republic of Panama, the official registering office in Panama City, but his complaint is not likely to be investigated. Another option would be to hire a Panamanian lawyer to bring suit against Mr. Kim in a criminal court in Panama, but since Panama is half a world away, this option is impractical.

In 1990, according to Lloyd's *Statistical Tables*, 4,748 ships of 100 gross tons or more were registered in Panama with a total gross tonnage of 62,184,000. Including ships of all sizes, Panama claims to have more than 12,000 ships in its registry.[6] Ship registration is a lucrative business for Panama, bringing in gross revenues to the governemnt of around $45 million each year and another $40 million to the Panamanian economy for various legal, technical, and financial support services. For years the directorate took little interest in a ship once it paid its registration fees and was given a registration number. Gradually, international pressure resulted in the directorate requiring some safety inspections, but there were still no provisions for monitoring living and working conditions on board. In an interview in 1984, the director general of the Panamanian registry, Hugo Torrijos, admitted that "social" conditions on Panamanian ships had been neglected. Panamanian maritime law had been written for coastal vessels staffed by Panamanian nationals. The relevance for international seafarers had not been considered. For years a new labor code was proposed and draft after draft circulated, but it was never adopted.

In 1982, the staff of the Center for Seafarers' Rights wrote a small booklet, *The Rights of Seafarers on Panamanian-Flag Ships*, based on the Panamanian labor code. Panamanian authorities praised the center for having succeeded with a project they had been planning for a long time. In fact the editing of the law had taken us only two days. The protection of foreign workers on their ships was obviously not high on the Panamanians' agenda.

Enlightened operators of ships registered in Panama who want to respect the rule of law on their ships and instill in their crews confidence that laws are being observed develop their policies in accordance with the labor law of Panama. But who enforces the law if the company does not voluntarily observe it? According to the directorate, inspectors in more than four hundred ports are ready to intervene on behalf of seafarers. I have found the system to be completely ineffective, however, as the following story elucidates.

In 1984, the Center for Seafarers' Rights received a series of complaints from seafarers working for the Carnival Cruise Line in Miami. When we got no satisfaction from the company, we called the directorate and asked for information about their inspector in Miami. The next time we were in Miami we phoned him and said that he had been recommended by the Panamanian office and that we wanted to talk to him about his work, to which he agreed. He listened intently as we described the problems as they had been told to us by the Carnival employees and finally exclaimed, "This sounds terrible. Who is going to investigate these complaints?" When we answered that we had been told this was his responsibility, he said that his job had nothing to do with crew conditions, only with equipment and safety. He suggested that perhaps the consul in Miami would be willing to look into the matter but added that the consul in Miami was ineffective and would do nothing unless a "brown envelope" were passed under the table.

There is virtually no way to enforce Panamanian labor law on Panamanian ships. This truth was underlined in two court cases in 1987 when the Republic of Panama sent experts into U.S. courts to testify that the law on the books was not necessarily applicable to non-Panamanian nationals and that "common maritime usage" sometimes took precedence over the general provisions of the law. The law is open to various interpretations depending on the customs of the nations involved.[7]

The following letter arrived in our office just before Christmas 1983:

> I would like to inform you that I am Mr. Erzon, age 29, holder of an Indonesian passport, and that I serve in the engine department of the Feoso Ambassador, a Panamanian flag ship At approximately 6:38 p.m. on 25 November our ship hit a rock in Qingdao harbor, after sailing from the same port. It

caused immediate leaking and the ship slopes. In case the ship cannot be used any more these are the questions we want to know about: (1) What are our rights under Panamanian and international law in case we are forced to resign? (2) When our rights are being denied, where can we contact a Panamanian consulate to present our claims?

On checking with the Panamanian maritime office, I learned that the authorities there were unaware of the accident. I was the first to tell them about it one month after it happened. When I related the questions the crew had asked, the authorities insisted they would follow up. Five months later, at the end of May, I received another letter from the *Feoso Ambassador*. It was still in the port of Qingdao, where fuel continued to leak into the harbor. It would soon be towed to the Philippines. All the members of the crew were being dismissed. They had heard nothing from any Panamanian authorities.

The humble Mauritian or Kiribati seafarer who works on a ship registered in Panama or Vanuatu or Cyprus or the Bahamas can hardly expect justice if he or she has a complaint. The Cayman Islands, one of the Commonwealth countries that is registering ships, has admitted that it was incapable of monitoring affairs on its ships in the past.

Some countries are not even aware of their responsibilities. In 1982, I phoned the administrator of the newly formed Bahamian international registry to ask about the situation of a particular seafarer. At the time the Bahamas was seeking to expand its fleet. The spontaneous reply from the head of the registry was, "My God, do we have to deal with that kind of problem, too?"

Ruben has another problem I have not yet mentioned. He is not receiving his full wages. In several ports he has received an "advance" of twenty dollars from the captain, but at no time in the past six months has he received all of his wages. Not including allotment payments, which may or may not have been forwarded to his account in Manila, he is owed more than five hundred dollars.

In many countries, Ruben has the right to sue for unpaid wages in the courts of the port state. While the ship is unloading in Port Everglades, Florida, for example, Ruben could demand that the captain pay 50 percent of the back wages.[8] If the demand were not met within a reasonable time, Ruben would have the right to hire a lawyer, who could put a lien on the ship to recover the wages. In practice, however, he would probably not succeed in finding a lawyer who would take on a case for such a small sum. The lawyer could not afford to undertake all the work involved to recover five hundred dollars, which, although it is a large sum to the seafarer, is not enough to pay the lawyer for his or her work. If the entire crew of the *Serrasalmo* were to join in the lien, the lawyer might be willing, but in this case Ruben is the only one who risks a court challenge.

There is another major barrier to legal action in Port Everglades. Before a lien can be put on a ship, the seafarer must post a forty thousand dollar bond. This administrative rule of the court system effectively eliminates any chance that seafarers will sue for back wages.

What about Ruben's complaint that he is being physically abused? Can the port state courts help him? Can he go to the police? The courts are reluctant to get involved in any internal dispute on a foreign ship, especially if there is the possibility of offending the flag state and appearing to be meddling in foreign affairs. In territorial waters, the port state can become involved if the security of the country or property is threatened, or if the public sensitivity is offended to the point of disturbing the peace.[9] The public would probably not be alarmed that Mr. Kim punches Ruben. If he were to murder him, however, the local criminal courts would take jurisdiction.[10]

Ruben's case introduces some of the basic principles and problems of port state control. The disastrous wreck of the *Torrey Canyon* in 1968 helps clarify the issues. When it spilled 117,000 tons of Kuwaiti crude oil on the shores of Cornwall and Brittany, the public suddenly became aware of the dangers inherent in merchant shipping and realized it was in the interest of a port state to extend its authority over what had been exclusively the concern of the flag state. With the current proliferation of flag states and their demonstrated inability or disinterest in enforcing minimum standards on their ships, port states will be all the more motivated to ensure that minimum standards are observed when ships visit their waters.

National laws are obviously inadequate in shipping, which is an extra-national industry, but what about international law? Is there some way international law can protect Ruben and others like him from being beaten up and enable them to get their back wages?

The International Labor Organization is the United Nations–related body that monitors and seeks to improve conditions for working people around the globe. It has been especially concerned with the welfare of seafarers at sea and in port. In its seventy years, 35 of the ILO's 166 conventions have pertained specifically to the living and working conditions of seafarers; and several others, relating to medical care and the right to organize, are relevant to seafarers even though they do not address them specifically.

Those ILO conventions pertaining to seafarers that have been ratified and are in force could form the basis of an international seafarers' law. Enforcement of the conventions however, remains the prerogative of the individual ratifying nations. Each ratifying nation must also pass the legislation necessary to implement the conventions. The individual seafarer who believes he or she is being denied the terms of a law has no practical way to appeal. The international law is only as effective as the political will of the member states to enforce it.

Panama has ratified Convention No. 68, for example, making it "responsible for the promotion of a proper standard of food supply and catering service for the crews in its seagoing vessels." But what does that mean to the seafarers on a Panamanian-registered vessel if Panama takes no intiative to enforce it? Before 1968, the ILO conventions, despite their international dimensions, were only as good as the shipowner's will to observe them. The situation improved somewhat in 1968, prompted in part by the *Torrey Canyon* disaster. At that time, the delegates to the ILO passed a minimum standards convention that incorporated eleven ILO conventions covering a range of issues facing seafarers, including their articles, medical care, repatriation, and officers' competency.[11]

One unique feature of the minimum standards convention, ILO No. 147, is its enforceability. Other conventions may be enforced only among nations that have ratified them. In the case of ILO No. 147, however, one nation can blow the whistle on another by complaining to the ILO in Geneva. This may result in improvements on the particular ship involved, but it has no permanent effect on the flag state's enforcement policy. If a ratifying nation has received a complaint or has other evidence that a ship calling in one of its ports is not meeting the standards of a convention, it may also take whatever steps are necessary, including delaying or detaining the ship, to rectify conditions on board "which are clearly hazardous to safety and health." Under the terms of ILO No. 147, a complaint may be initiated "by a member of the crew, ... or any person with an interest in ... safety and health hazards to its crew."

ILO No. 147 is an important document. The port state has taken over some of the responsibility once reserved exclusively for the flag state. This change in enforcement jurisdiction reflects the opinion that flag states were inadequately enforcing standards on their ships.

Soon after ILO Convention No. 147 was adopted, eight European countries—Belgium, Denmark, France, the Federal Republic of Germany, the Netherlands, Norway, Sweden, and the United Kingdom—met to see what else port states could do to enforce standards. On March 2, 1978, the maritime authorities of these countries met at the Hague to sign the Hague Memorandum of Understanding on Port State Control (MOUPSC), the purpose of which was to ensure that ILO No. 147 and other international conventions were taken seriously.

Their concern was timely. Fifteen days later the *Amoco Cadiz* ripped open on Brittany's rocky coast, spilling 300,000 tons of crude oil, polluting beaches, and devastating animal life. The disaster made safety at sea an even more urgent issue. Coincidentally, the accident occurred on the first World Maritime Day, whose theme was "Safer Ships on Cleaner Oceans." Europe was outraged that a single ship could do so much property damage, and clearly the flag state bore some of the blame for the ship's lax safety standards.

Eventually fourteen countries signed the Memorandum of Understanding on Port State Control, agreeing that seven maritime conventions (six from the International Maritime Organization relating to safety and one from the International Labor Organization relating to living and working conditions) would be mutually enforced.[12] Inspectors from each state would board 25 percent of the ships entering its ports to ensure that they conformed to standards. Inspections were to be on a random basis, and no flags were to be discriminated against. Substandard ships would be delayed or detained until they conformed. Because uneven enforcement would allow unfair competition between ports, all ports were urged to work together.

Maritime experts the world over acknowledge that the memorandum has contributed to improved safety, living, and working conditions on ships entering ports in Europe. And because of the way the program is administered, far more than 25 percent of all ships are inspected. Once a ship has been inspected it will not be reinspected for at least six months. Inspectors will search for other ships. By this means, most ships calling regularly in Europe are inspected in the course of a year, and those that are deficient are usually detained until they meet international standards.

There are, however, a few exceptions, as the following case illustrates. On June 5, 1986, a five-thousand–ton general-cargo vessel, the *Mount Data*, flying the flag of the Philippines, was inspected in Vlissingen, Holland, on behalf of the MOUPSC by Hans de Vries of the Netherlands Shipping Inspection Bureau. He made a list of sixty defects and deficiencies, most of them related to safety: lifeboats could not be launched; neither the line-throwing mechanisms nor the emergency lighting on deck worked; fire hoses were torn; bilge pumps were inoperative; maps were outdated; and there were no health certificates on board. According to de Vries, the seafarers had received only one meal a day for several days and were pale and weak. He intended to call for a doctor from the state health service. On the day of the inspection, crew members themselves had contributed a total of eighty dollars for food, but what they could buy would barely hold them over during the three-day sail to Gijón, Spain.

De Vries left the ship at six in the evening after ordering its arrest under the terms of the Memorandum of Understanding. By the time he reached land, the ship was already sailing away. Commenting on the incident, de Vries said that during his seven years with the Netherlands Shipping Inspection Bureau, six hundred ships had been arrested but only once before had a ship escaped. He said that before the MOUPSC was in effect, "floating coffins" often came to the Netherlands. With port state control, they generally avoided Europe altogether.

Certificates and visual inspections can verify that standards for hulls and equipment, fire safety, and officer competence are being met. Port inspectors do not address many of the seafarers' greatest needs, however. In some cases, the problems are theoretically covered by the memorandum but the inspectors are unable to do anything about them. Articles of agreement, for example, are required according to the memorandum, but since the failure to sign articles is not directly hazardous to the health and safety of the vessel, it is not an offense warranting its delay or detention. In other cases, the problems lie outside the mandate of the inspections. Inspectors have no authority to deal with wage problems, for example.

Many of the provisions of ILO No. 147, the Minimum Standards Convention, contain vague language, requiring a subjective evaluation on the part of the inspector: "cleanliness," "adequate security," "decently habitable accommodations." Recognizing both the seriousness of "living and working" deficiencies and the difficulty of making objective judgments, the secretariat that administers the MOUPSC is determined to develop realistic criteria for evaluation consistent with the intention of the authors of the conventions. The 1987 annual report of the secretariat describes an initiative to "intensify, where possible, port state control with regard to seafarers' living and working conditons." The challenge from the secretariat's perspective is to expand the range of ILO requirements that can be inspected "objectively."

Another problem is exemplified by article 22 of the 1978 IMO International Convention on Standards of Training, Certification and Watchkeeping for Seafarers. It recognizes that "not only safe operation of the ship and its equipment but also good human relationships between the seafarers on board would greatly enhance the safety of life at sea." The article "invites governments (1) to establish or encourage the establishment of training programs aimed at safeguarding good human relationships on board; and (2) to take adequate measures to minimize any element of loneliness and isolation for crew members on board ships." The article, profound in its implications, has never been implemented, although various studies have been initiated.

The Memorandum of Understanding allows for citizen participation in the enforcement process: "Any person or organization with a legitimate interest in the safe operation of the ship [and] shipboard living and working conditions [may request an inspection] . . . if there are clear grounds for believing that the ship does not substantially meet the requirements of a relevant instrument."[13] Administrators of the memorandum have been very responsive when seafarers or port workers or chaplains have phoned the headquarters in the Netherlands asking that a particular ship be inspected.

Seafarers who have been reluctant to ask for an inspection, for fear of reprisals, have turned to chaplains or union officials, who in turn have asked for the inspection.

Despite its "subjective" limitations, ILO No. 147 provides several specific "new" protections that should be taken seriously by inspectors in countries where the convention has been ratified. These include, as established in Conventions No. 55, 56, and 130, provision for medical care in the event a seafarer becomes ill or injured. Presumably an inspector could determine that the owner takes responsibility for providing such care. Likewise, ILO No. 147 requires that the shipowner provide every seafarer with articles and enumerates the items to be included. The secretariat can instruct inspectors to verify that each seafarer has signed articles, but there is no penalty for noncompliance.

I have not forgotten Ruben. I wish he could find a sympathetic MOUPSC inspector in Europe who could justify investigating Ruben's human relations complaints. I would like to challenge the secretariat that oversees the MOUPSC to take his complaint seriously, for humanitarian reasons and because the safety of his ship is jeopardized by the inhuman actions of the second engineer. ILO No. 147 does not cover wage issues. A MOUPSC inspector cannot help Ruben with this issue. We say good-bye to Ruben, hoping he will find a sympathetic union representative or a port chaplain who will advocate for him in securing his unpaid wages. There is no effective legal remedy. His problem is complicated by the fact that the Filipino Association for Mariner's Employment wants all Filipino seafarers to settle all complaints in Filipino courts and to avoid foreign courts completely. Ruben is caught in a conflict of laws. He could well repeat what Starbuck said in *Moby Dick*, "I stand alone here upon the open sea with two oceans and a whole continent between me and the law. Aye, aye, 'tis so."[14]

Shipowners have not put the welfare of seafarers high on their agenda. While most of the industry acknowledges that someone should be concerned with the human "element," to use a degrading term, or "hands," certainly not an adequate description of a human being, the task is usually left to do-gooders or well-meaning academics.

The situation is worse now than at any time since World War II. Profits are the only rudder guiding the course of the maritime industry. In recent years maritime fraud has reached alarming proportions. There was a time when the maritime industry prided itself on its high degree of trust. A handshake could seal a deal of a million dollars. Today a different mood prevails. Teams of lawyers pore over every document searching for loopholes, or means of escape from the terms of their commitments; ethical standards have collapsed; and fraud is rampant—further evidence of the anachronism that results when national states try to control a transnational industry.

The United Nations Commission on Trade and Development, along with other organizations, has been investigating the problem of maritime fraud for years.[15] These investigations all concern cargoes and property. If major corporations are able to defraud each other even though they have large legal departments, how much more vulnerable are individual seafarers. To my knowledge there has been no investigation, despite frequent complaints, on behalf of seafarers who were defrauded by a ship's operators.

Seafarers are legally a group set apart from other members of the work force. Thus, not only do they not enjoy the same freedoms as their sisters and brothers who work on shore by virtue of having to live and work far from home and community, but they have also sometimes been treated as inferior human beings by the courts.

It is more than coincidence that Judge William Scott Stowell, the leading British admiralty judge, and Justice Joseph Story, who wrote the original U.S. maritime decisions, made similar declarations about the legal status of seafarers.[16] Story's paternalism was built on his firm conviction that seafarers were irresponsible by nature and disadvantaged as a class of workers. They had no right to vote and few advocates in the political arena. In *Hardin v. Gordon*, he defined seafarers as wards of admiralty. In *Brown v. Lull*, he further defined their incompetence.

> Seamen are a class of persons remarkable for their rashness, thoughtlessness and improvidence. They are generally necessitous, ignorant of the nature and extent of their own rights and privileges, and for the most part incapable of duly appreciating their value. They combine, in a singular manner, the apparent anomalies of gallantry, extravagance, profusion in expenditure, indifference to the future, credulity, which is easily won, and confidence, which is readily surprised. Hence it is, that bargains between them and shipowner, the latter being persons of great intelligence and shrewdness in business, are deemed open to much observation and scrutiny; for they involve great inequality of knowledge, of forecast, of power, and of conditions. Courts of admiralty on this account are accustomed to consider seamen as peculiarly entitled to their protection so that they have been by a somewhat bold figure, often said to be favorites of courts of admiralty. In a just sense they are so, so far as the maintenance of their rights, and the protection of their interests against the effects of the superior skill and shrewdness of master and owners of ships are concerned.[17]

As the American legal system unfolded, laws ostensibly intended to protect seafarers often had the opposite effect. Being a ward of the court was not necessarily a benefit. The situation in England was similar. Leo Barnes, in his study of British maritime law as it applied to Indian seamen, wrote that "whatever provisions were made in law apparently for the benefit of the seamen were in fact jeopardizing the interests of seamen."[18]

The 1790 American Seamen's Act is a case in point. It required that all masters provide seafarers with articles of agreement. A master who failed in this responsibility was to pay the seafarer a wage equal to the highest wage that had been paid to any seafarer in that port in the previous three months. Further, the master was fined twenty dollars, half of which was for the lawyer who prosecuted the case. The articles had to include the hour at which the seafarer was to report and to state that whoever did not show up on time forfeited a day's pay for every hour he was late. If the seafarer failed to show up altogether, or deserted after showing up, he not only forfeited any advanced wages he had received but had to pay the master an equivalent amount as punishment. Under some circumstances, if he continued to refuse to sail, he could be imprisoned until he paid. Thus a law that appeared to guarantee a seafarer the right to articles ended up being a statute that allowed a master to imprison him for desertion.

There was another double-edged sword in the law, relating to safety. If before sailing or once the ship had sailed, the majority of the crew together with the mate decided the ship was unsafe or ill equipped, they had the right to dispatch two of their number to a judge or a justice of the peace. That judge would then appoint a committee of three experts to evaluate the complaints. If two out of the three agreed with the complaint, repairs could be required, and costs fell to the master. If the experts did not agree with the complaint, damages for detaining the ship and for its inspection were deducted from the seafarers' salaries. Ostensibly, the law protected the safety of the crew, but the severity of the punishment for bad judgment or for holding to a standard of safety that was higher than the judge's inspectors could discourage a crew from acting.

Throughout the nineteenth century the rights of owners and agents were more often protected than those of seafarers. Laws that appeared to favor seafarers were soon replaced by other laws.

In February 1895, Congress passed the Maguire Act, abolishing imprisonment for desertion in the coastal trade. Believing it was their right, four seamen traveling along the Pacific Coast en route to South America left their ship, which they thought was unsafe, at a West Coast port. The court said that, although the ship visited several ports along the West Coast, it was not considered to be in the coastal trade, and the four were imprisoned for nine months as deserters. The case was appealed to the Supreme court, where it aroused public interest and ultimately public indignation. Justice Henry Billings wrote for the majority:

> *Indeed seamen are treated by Congress, as well as by the Parliament of Great Britain, as deficient in that full and intelligent responsiblity for their acts which is accredited to ordinary adults, and as needing the protection of the law in the same sense which minors and wards are entitled to the protection of their parents and guardians. . . . In the face of this legislation upon the subject of desertion and absence without leave, which was in force in this country for more than sixty years before the 13th Amendment [abolishing slavery] was adopted and similar legislation abroad from time immemorial, it cannot be open to doubt that the provision against involuntary servitude was never intended to apply to their contracts.*[19]

The slaves had been freed but not seafarers.

"They treat us like slaves" is still a frequent refrain on ships. Seafarers still do not have adequate legal protection. The question is, Can the world community develop an enforceable international law for seafarers? Can maritime labor law, which traditionally moves very slowly, keep pace with the needs of a changing maritime world?

The Maltese ambassador to the United Nations, Arvid Pardo, first proposed a new attitude toward the sea in a historic address to the General Assembly on November 1, 1967. He expressed the view that insofar as the oceans are the common heritage of all humankind, they could lead to a new way of thinking about the globe's resources and about how people interact with one another in using those resources.

In the Law of the Sea Convention that evolved, several principles emerged: the sea can be used by all but not owned by any; all users are to cooperate in the ocean's management; and profits from its use are to be shared by all. As Elisabeth

Mann Borgese has written, "The oceans are our great laboratory for the making of a new international order."[20]

I am sure the authors of the Law of the Sea Convention were thinking primarily of the resources that come from the sea when they wrote the law. But what about those who work on the sea? Will seafarers benefit from this new international order, or will they continue to be players in a script written in an age of exploitation of human and natural resources?

SIX

The Stresses of Seafaring

A SHIP has been called a "total institution."[1] As in a prison or a convent or a boarding school, one lives and works and all one's needs are met in the same confined space. Ships are an extreme example of a structure that is isolated from the rest of the world. Except for an occasional supply of food and fuel, the shipboard community is completely self-reliant, an independent society that generates its own power, distills its own water, and disposes of its wastes.

What kind of person elects a life of such isolation? What are the human costs—social and psychological—of life on a merchant ship?

There are volumes of research on who goes to sea and why, which needs are met and which are denied, but the majority of these studies were conducted before the seafaring population was so predominantly Asian. Social structures and cultural expectations are different in economically developing countries, and these studies, focused as they are on Western seafarers, do not necessarily describe today's maritime work force. There has been very little systematic research on Asian and other Third World seafarers.[2]

One might expect that a carefully developed screening

process would be used to ensure that the qualifications and aptitudes of potential seafarers are suited to the realities of shipboard existence. If one were going to live in a space station with a dozen other people for as long as a year at a time, there would be extensive physical and psychological testing. Some Eastern European nations have developed procedures to help determine who is best suited to life at sea, but countries in the Third World have no such screening process.[3] A seafarer discovers only after taking a job whether he or she is suited for seafaring, and by then it is often too late to make a change. As should be clear by now, the reasons for becoming a mariner are often irrelevant to the job itself.

In Burma (Myanmar), for example, seafarers are recruited from among the sons of military and government employees and wealthy citizens. Burma is rather closed to the rest of the world, and seafaring is one way to escape the isolation. A privileged occupation, seafaring has been reserved for those in power or for those who have one thousand dollars or more to pay the informal recruiting fee. Seafarers from Burma enjoy many benefits, including freedom from income taxes, and money earned on ships can be legally exchanged for kyat at the real rate rather than at the official rate, a difference of 700 percent. Whether these privileged young men are appropriate candidates for a job at sea is not considered in the selection process and often there is considerable disparity between what they expect and the job itself. Burmese crew often discover that life has ill prepared them for chipping paint and wiping grease.

The factors determining whether someone chooses a seafaring career differ from country to country in the Third World. As we have seen, the primary reason is to make more money than one can on shore. Those in a position to make that choice, however, may not make the best seafarers.

Only in those countries where more money can be made at sea than on shore is seafaring a relatively high-status job. As we have seen, as soon as Koreans could earn equivalent wages at home, they left seagoing careers. Several of the sixteen maritime training centers in Korea have been forced to move to China, and the Korean Maritime University in Pusan is having trouble finding candidates. The profession has lost its glamour. It is said that fewer people want to marry seafarers now that their earnings are no longer enough of a compensation for the long absences. Those people who joined the merchant service to see the world can now afford to go as tourists.

Seafaring continues to be a respected job in the Philippines, and there is considerable community support for the men and women who go to sea. In towns such as Anini-y in Antique province, most young men look forward to a career at sea, and the town prospers from the incomes of its seagoing sons and daughters. Many Filipino young people regard seafaring as a way to break out of the cycle of poverty, to earn money to start a business, to pay off their debts, to educate their dependents, or to buy land. Most seafarers come from the middle class, and many have some college education.[4] They see a job at sea as an opportunity to improve their economic status and that of their families. Once on board ship, however, the highly motivated young people become restless with the routine labors. What looks like a glamorous job from outside proves to be quite unglamorous. Encouraged by plans to return eventually to shore and pursue another career, most Filipinos, like other young seafarers, find they can put up with the life for a few years.

In India, work roles are highly differentiated, and certain jobs are reserved for certain social classes. Traditionally, most ratings come from seafaring families, but attitudes are changing and modern workers resent the strict roles. Many crew members who are recruited are not content with the old structures: "The master-servant relationship ... is much resented by 'modernized' ratings who are conscious of their rights and privileges. ... Mutual distrust and humiliation results in active as well as passive hostility and feelings of resentment."[5]

Most enthusiastic and highly motivated seafarers initially

adjust to the adverse conditions at sea in anticipation of another career, but over time, beginning a new career proves increasingly difficult. In poor countries such as India, Indonesia, Bangladesh, and the Philippines, where unemployment is especially high, it is not easy for a seafarer to find a job on shore, and entry-level jobs pay far less than the seafarer has been earning. In India, going to work on shore represents a loss of up to 75 percent of a seafarer's earnings.

Often the only choice is to return to sea. As time goes by and the prospect of a "normal" life on shore has dimmed, the seafarers become more embittered by the hardships and separations of shipboard life; the resentments are no longer mitigated by the prospect of a normal life in the future.

Not only have recruiting agencies given little or no consideration to hiring men and women who are well suited to the job, but there seems to be little or no thought given to hiring workers of similar or compatible cultures and nationalities. On many ships, the seafarers work well together even though they are from half a dozen different nations. But on others, the differences in language, race, and religion lead to stress and serious misunderstandings. I once met a lonely Punjabi Sikh who for a year had shared no language in common with anyone on board his ship. He was devastated by the experience. It is not difficult to do one's job in this situation, but the lack of social contact is very stressful. Traditions are so established that as a third engineer he knew at once on coming to the ship how to find his cabin, which shift he was to work, what he was to do, and even where he was to sit in the messroom. He could perform his job satisfactorily, but he could barely endure the lack of human relationships.

Koreans are one of the world's most homogeneous people and typically have not had much experience working with people of other cultures. Interpersonal relationships are highly structured and fragile in Korean society. When this structure is disturbed, the result is often serious distress. In 1987, the *Green Star* had an all-Korean crew, but morale was very low and there was excessive drinking and fighting. After observing the crew, a port chaplain concluded that the captain was not exercising his traditional authority. He may have been technically competent, but he lacked the leadership qualities that were essential to the operation of a ship crewed by people from a hierarchical society. The leadership vacuum had led to a deterioration of the entire operation.

Normally an all-Korean crew will work well together, but mixing Koreans with people of other nationalities can lead to dislocation. Disruption of the complex social relationships among Korean seafarers can result in withdrawal or illness and, if there is no other emotional release for the tensions, violence.

A chaplain in New Jersey observed an Indian captain reprimanding a Korean seafarer in the presence of the all-Korean ratings. The reprimand, for a rather minor offense, might have gone almost unnoticed, but it was a devastating rebuke to the Korean. He lost face and became almost dysfunctional, was unable to eat, and had severe stomach cramps. The captain had no idea that his rebuke would have such an effect. Eleven of the other thirteen crew members also developed stomach problems—at least two from bleeding ulcers—apparently as a result of the stress caused by the cultural differences between the Indians officers and the Korean crew.

Because fewer Koreans are going to sea than in the past, recruiting agents in Korea are having to mix Korean seafarers with seafarers of other nationalities. Despite a history of animosities, Japanese officers have successfully led Korean crews, perhaps because the Koreans are especially eager to impress the Japanese with their competence and because the cultures are similar. There is an area in China where there are approximately 2 million Koreans; the Chinese here speak Korean and are sensitive to Koreans' needs. Recruiting agents are hopeful that Korean officers and Chinese ratings from this area will be able to work cooperatively with one another. Such a consciousness of cultural needs is the exception, however, among recruiters. Generally there is little awareness of incompatibility.

Insensitivity to the superstitions of other cultures is a cause of profound misunderstanding and stress on ships with mixed crews, and superstitions can run deep. One day the chief officer on the *Blue Arrow* found the body of the cook hanging from a pipe in his cabin. Believing that the ghosts of suicide victims become angry and vengeful, the crew became virtually immobilized with fear. The Western captain was totally at a loss as to what to do. No one would walk by the cook's cabin, and his neighbors moved to other rooms. The second cook refused to enter the freezer. All the ship's lights were kept on day and night. The chief officer was especially paranoid.

Finally, a chaplain who understood the culture of the seafarers worked with the crew to purify the room and rid the ship of the ghost. In an intense service of prayers for the deceased cook and his family, the chaplain was able to assure the crew that the demons had been exorcized. The crew wrote and signed a letter of comfort to the family, and the cook's cabin was converted into a chapel, where a memorial service was held. Members of the crew were freed of their fears, and the ship resumed normal operations under the command of an amazed and grateful captain.

Competent management calls for research into the cultural needs of a crew before it is hired as a way to prevent misunderstandings that can interfere with peace of mind and productivity. People who are raised on the Pacific islands of the Maldives or Tuvalu, for example, are not automatically comfortable on technologically sophisticated ships. A group of five seafarers from Kiribati reported that, having no idea how to release their seat belts after their flight to meet their first ship, one of the men took a knife and cut the belts, freeing himself and his colleagues.

Another group from Kiribati had never been on an elevator and understandably refused to enter one. Ahead of the group, three men had walked into the car and the doors had closed.

When the doors opened again the three men had disappeared, without a trace.

Chaplains and ship visitors point to cultural combinations that appear to cause difficulties. Greeks tend to be expressive in a way that appears contentious and pugnacious to Asians, and Norwegians tend to be impassive in a way that others may see as unfriendly and even hostile.

Communication failures can be distressful for all concerned. On the banana ship the *Atlantic Ocean*, the crew worked well together and morale was good until a new captain came aboard. One day he publicly reprimanded the Filipino electrician. The electrician was humiliated and immediately offered to resign. The captain was surprised but accepted the resignation, and the electrician was replaced. The electrician had resigned not because of what he had done or because he wanted to leave the ship but because the captain had humiliated him. The captain had no idea.

In another case, a security guard called a chaplain for help in dealing with four unruly Sri Lankans from a Greek ship. On arrival in port, the chaplain learned that the Sri Lankans had been denied shore passes. The guard had been posted at the gangway to keep them from leaving the ship, but they had slipped past him and turned themselves in at the security gate, saying they would rather go to prison than remain on the ship. After lengthy discussions, the chaplain learned that the chief engineer had slapped one of them. The Sri Lankans would have given up their careers and gone to jail rather than continue to work under what they saw as abusive conditions. The chaplain persuaded the Sri Lankans to return to the ship on the condition that they would be repatriated, which they were the next day. The Greek officers never did understand the problem and continued to assume that the Sri Lankans were "sissies" who lacked manly virtues.

Some of the stresses at sea can never be eliminated. Significant progress has been made in the design of cabins and living space, but a ship is still a powerful and awesome machine with mechanical liabilities. Noise and vibration are less of a problem than in the past, but the noise in the engine room can still be stressful. In a 1988 survey of Korean seafarers, 84 percent objected to the noise and vibration on board.[6]

Seafarers have complained to me about fumes, dust, and dirt. Toxic fumes from hazardous cargoes can be especially disturbing. There are many tales of seafarers being overcome by fumes while cleaning unventilated cargo holds. Often neither the officers nor the crew understand the chemical properties of the bulk and liquid cargo.

Most stress-related problems can be mitigated if management is conscientious. Changes in temperature and climate are often frequent and extreme, yet some operators make no provision to protect their crews from the effect of these changes. Crews from the tropics, for example, often do not think to bring heavy clothing or cannot afford them. It is not unusual to see seafarers shivering because neither they nor the operators brought along appropriate clothes.

Divisions between departments can also cause considerable stress. In a crew of twenty people, fifteen may be at different salary scales—a sign of the many divisions and inequalities on board. The chief engineer earns a little less than the captain, the first assistant engineer less than the chief officer, and on down the line. The steward's department is on a different salary scale altogether. Rivalries and jealousies, especially between the deck department and the engine department, undermine teamwork. Many engineers believe that their skills are equal or even superior to those of the navigating officers, who do not understand the technical operation, yet the navigating staff give the orders and are regarded as the "real" seafarers.

Other conditions foster separation between officers and ratings. Traditionally, the two groups eat and socialize in separate spaces. It need not be so. I once boarded a Norwegian vessel on which a young black man was carrying a small white child along the companionway. In the mess hall the entire crew was sitting together around family tables. There were men, women, and children. I asked one of the women about her husband's job on board. She promptly corrected me. She was the second officer and her husband and son were traveling for a month as the guests of the company. Contracts for the entire mixed-nationality crew were for four months on and two months off. There were weekly staff meetings, and, except for the skeletal staff which was operating the ship, the entire crew attended. When I expressed my surprise and pleasure at the whole arrangement, a crew member commented, with reserve, "Why not make life on board ship as pleasant as possible?"

Such attitudes are extremely rare. In many situations the officers feel compelled to maintain a social distance from the crew. Captain Spyro Nissiotis on the *White Raven* told the chaplain, "If we get friendly with them, they will not obey our orders." One captain insisted on always wearing a uniform to intimidate his crew, all of whom were from the Third World. Crews in turn feel that the dignity of the work is diminished by the superior attitudes of the officers. Blanche Barnes concludes that "the mutual distrust between the officers and the ratings is the root cause of the majority of problems and conflicts on board the ship."[7]

Much of the work on a ship is boring and routine. During a typical four-hour shift, the navigating officer sometimes has little to do, while the engineer has to do no more than watch the dials. For some, the most important piece of equipment is the teapot. Deck ratings spend day after day chipping paint and repainting. In view of the educational level of today's Asian seafarers, such work represents a depreciation of their skills and aptitudes. One of the stated goals of the Philippine Overseas Employment Administration's policy of sending workers abroad is to help them improve their skills, but in many cases the opposite has occurred. Overqualified and underemployed, they become frustrated.

As staffing levels are reduced, the boredom and routine become coupled with work overload, especially on shorter voyages. The amount of overtime required of some officers tests their endurance almost to the breaking point. Given that a ship never stops working during its time at sea, in any emergency the safety of crew and ship depend on the captain and senior officers, who are never relieved of their responsibilities.

Even being docked in port does not offer relief. The work routine continues. Officers are responsible for unloading and reloading, for stores and repairs, and for attending to paperwork and formalities in port. With only a few hours to turn around, the seafarers often have time to do no more for themselves than make a phone call. One captain told me that in seventeen visits to the Port of New York and New Jersey, he had never had the opportunity to leave the dock area.

Seafarers sign on for a specific voyage or for a specific length of time and have no guarantee of another job when the voyage is over. By contrast, employees in shore-based jobs can look forward to the possibility of years or even lifetimes of steady employment with one company. Some shipping companies have objected to the constant turnover and have instituted a system of crew continuity so they can count on having the same work force. In the majority of cases, however, seafarers, especially those from the Third World, are unemployed when their contracts are over. They do not expect to return to the same ship in the same position. Many must start a job search all over again. Despite their skills and experience, they are hired as casual workers.

Because the waiting periods between jobs are often long, seafarers may actually work only ten or fifteen years in the course of twenty years of sea service. During the idle time, they have to stretch their income,[8] and during the months when they are under articles, they have to try to save in anticipation of the long months of unemployment. Filipino studies show that most overseas workers are unable to accumulate the capital they need, forcing them to borrow between jobs against expected earnings.[9] Thus, just as in the days of the crimps, many seafarers are economic hostages to a life at sea.

Seafarers tend to mask their feelings about the threats of dangerous weather, serious storms, and disasters, but they often reach shore with frayed nerves and their courage seriously challenged. No profession has as many industrial accidents and deaths as seafaring, and even the most modern and "safe" vessels have been known to disappear without a trace.[10] To understand the problem fully, one must take into account the responsibility of registries, classification societies, and insurers as well as maritime schools, ship managers, and others.

Cutthroat industrywide competition inevitably leads to lower standards. Replacing career seafarers with less qualified newcomers jeopardizes the overall level of competence. Cutting the size of the crew means there is less time for onboard maintenance, which threatens safety. At the same time corners are being cut in shore-side maintenance. Many registries provide fewer safety inspections and contract with classification societies to conduct the surveys that determine seaworthiness. Classification societies, such as Lloyd's Registry and the American Bureau of Shipping, are private businesses in competition with one another. If their inspections are too strict, a shipowner may be tempted to use a classification society that is more lenient. Recently, one registry claimed that the classification societies were being too stringent in their safety inspections and threatened to establish its own classification society that would award a first-class rating without such thorough inspections. Furthermore, insurance companies pay little attention to safety on board. In fact, they offer an alternative to the maintenance of safety by paying in the event of a loss.

Equipment failure accounts for only a small percentage of the accidents at sea. Most are caused by the people on board and ashore. No matter how demanding inspections may be, if maritime management continues to neglect the human needs of seafarers, accidents will continue to occur. As far as seafarers themselves are concerned, equipment failure, natural dangers at sea, and the threat of fires on board pale in comparison to their worries about living and working conditions.

U.S. courts have recognized that a ship is not seaworthy if it does not provide safe conditions for each seafarer on board. If the ventilation system is inoperable, for example, affecting the seafarers' health, then the ship is not seaworthy and the deterioration of the seafarers' health can be blamed on the shipowner who overlooked the deficiency.[11]

Separation from family and community is another ongoing cause of stress for seafarers, and most experience free-floating anxiety about life at home. On average, the contract on oceangoing vessels is for a longer period of time now than it was in the recent past. In the 1970s, when labor unions had more influence in the maritime industry, contracts were for six or nine months, sometimes less. Today the average time at sea is a year or more, making family, community, and interpersonal life all but impossible. Officers occasionally invite their spouses or sweethearts to accompany them, but working spouses often cannot afford the time, and others find the time at sea so boring that they prefer to remain at home. Not being able to nurture one's children or offer support during a family crisis can cause serious stress. The Center for Seafarers' Rights recently received an anguished letter from a seafarer detailing his dilemma. He had just learned that his wife had been in a serious accident requiring hospitalization and therapy. Should he go home to be with her, he asked, or remain on board to pay for her cure? He could not do both.

In May 1990 I received the following letter posted in Durban, South Africa:

> I am the father of four daughters, all are married. My wife lives alone in Calcutta. On April 19 I received a shocking telex on board that my second daughter had been cruelly burnt to death by her husband. This message reached me so late (after

ten days) and my ship was in mid-Atlanta Ocean. I was unable to contact my wife. I have no further information and I cannot imagine how much my wife suffers alone at home as I do on this vessel. I am also much distressed about my granddaughter of four years old, who lost her mother in her innocent childhood. My financial commitments are so crucial that I am looking for help and moral support.

When seafarers are away for a year or more, the family learns to function without them. Their role at home is unclear, and they feel awkward. Having suffered from homesickness while on board, they soon look forward to returning to the ship, where their role is well defined and necessary.

Prolonged periodic separations from family and community have led seafarers to experience increased feelings of alienation. Some, especially in the West, drop out of society altogether. Miriam Sherar wrote a passionate book while she was trying to salvage her troubled marriage to a seafarer. She begins one chapter with quotations from classified ads that have appeared in maritime union newspapers. The ads poignantly summarize the failure of family relationships:

> *Your wife passed away in October. Very important that you contact.*

> *Please call home immediately concerning your baby's eye operation.*

> *Your wife asks that you get in touch with her as soon as possible.*

> *If anyone has any information on the whereabouts of . . . , please contact his wife.*

> *Your son, Frank, Jr., is getting married. He is hopeful that you can attend the wedding.*[12]

Chaplains often talk with seafarers about their loss of physical relations as a result of the long periods of isolation. Sexual deprivation is clearly one of the dehumanizing aspects of shipboard life.

Serious illnesses often result from the stress of dealing with contract problems, intercultural conflicts, difficult and some-times dangerous living and working conditions, job insecurity, and separation from family and community. In studying the effects of stress on Indian seafarers, Blanche Barnes discovered that even the younger seafarers who were able to adjust to the difficult conditions experienced measurable deterioration of ego strength after only a few months at sea. After a few years many had symptoms of serious stress-related illnesses. The navigating officers were susceptible to the so-called ex-ecutive diseases—high blood pressure, coronary heart dis-ease, and diabetes—and the navigating ratings manifested a higher than normal incidence of bronchitis, asthma, colds, coughs, and tuberculosis.[13] In many cases the stress contrib-uted to nicotine and alcohol dependency, which in turn contributed to health disorders. Getting adequate amounts of exercise is also very difficult in the confines of a ship.

Engine room workers are less susceptible to disease than navigating officers but still have higher than normal incidences of ulcers and skin rashes. In addition, accidents are common in both departments. Officers are more likely to get sick than ratings, but only a small percentage of the personnel are free from health problems caused by their inability to adjust to the hostile conditions on board or the severe psychosocial deprivation.

Rather than helping, management often contributes to the seafarers' adjustment problems.

Barnes reviewed the backgrounds and ego strength of each of the seafarers she interviewed to determine whether the person was likely to react to stress regardless of where he or she worked or whether specific conditions at sea con-tributed to the physical and mental deterioration. Barnes found that a control group of shore-based workers showed very few of the same symptoms.

Some of the seafarers Barnes studied adjusted well to shipboard life, but the vast majority did not. After only four months, even the seafarers with stable backgrounds who began their jobs well motivated and optimistic, showed signs of deterioration. Poor health contributed to poorer performance, absenteeism, apathy, and a greater than average likelihood of being in an accident. Barnes concluded that "overall mental health adjustment, personality integration and ego strength potential of seafaring personnel have been adversely affected by the demands of a maritime profession."[14]

A study of Filipino sailors conducted by Balthazar V. Reyes and Alma Lucindo-Jimenez corroborates Barnes's findings. Their study found that a higher than normal percentage of seafarers showed evidence of psychiatric disorders. The researchers attributed their finding to the seafarers' inability to deal openly with their stress.[15]

In view of the conditions on board ship, do any seafarers like their job? The answer depends somewhat on who is asking and under what circumstances. Mary Brooks found that a majority of seafarers from Southeast Asian nations were satisfied, but she also admitted that some of her information came from unemployed seafarers who were trying to please recruiting agents.[16] According to Barnes, only 12 percent of the officers in her sample said they really liked their job. Overall, 68 percent of the crew members on board were dissatisfied and would have liked to leave merchant service. A resounding 87 percent of the ratings, many of whom came from seafaring families, said they would never permit their children to take such an intolerable job.[17]

A captain with a Hong Kong company described the situation as follows:

> Changes at sea have brought about a decline in amenities, recreational areas, food, cleanliness, and, in real terms, wages. There is an increased work load, shorter stays in ports, and berths that are often miles from recreational facilities. Consequently very few people actually want or enjoy a life at sea. We comprise a reluctant workforce; we must leave our families for most of a year, often we are unable to communicate because of language difficulties, and we have no rights or representation; we are abused by shore officials and shore regulations, treated as second-class citizens ashore, working for people we often never

see, who have never seen a ship and who regard us as a piece
of machinery of the ship. Couple this with the fact that we
work in one of the highest danger industries in the world with
no real access to medical care.[18]

A ship's captain has a nigh-impossible job. He is caught between the crew, with whom he often has basic sympathies, because he was one of them before being promoted, and the shipowner, for whom he is now the agent on board. His responsibilities are heavy, and he is often alone in pursuit of them. A report from a Scandinavian captain on a large ship crewed entirely by Koreans told of having no one to talk with for months at a time. He did not like the Korean food, so he had set up a little galley in his cabin, where he survived on "caviar and crispbreads." He was a recluse on his own ship.[19]

In the days of sailing ships, the captain was often part owner of the vessel and was clearly in charge, making crewing and navigation and sometimes business decisions. "My ship, my order" was his undisputed claim. The captain still bears the weight of responsibility for the safe navigation of the ship and for the well-being of the crew, but his power to fulfill these responsibilities has been seriously eroded. As vessels have become mechanized, the captain has had to depend on the expertise of engineers to propel them. Business decisions are made on shore. All the captain has to do is follow orders, some of which are given by people who do not understand the realities of ocean navigation.

The technological sophistication of some of today's vessels can be overwhelming for captains who are masters at dead reckoning and the use of the sextant but unfamiliar with computers. Modern captains must be regularly retrained as new and more complicated collision-avoidance systems and advanced radar-plotting aids are developed. Younger seafarers who are more adept at computers can threaten the captain's job security. Some captains have expressed their preference for ships from earlier days, which were more "user-friendly."

There are times when captains disagree with the instructions they are receiving by telex and fax from the manager to whom they are responsible. Captain Philip Cheek in *Legacies of Peril* tells of many instances in which he was required to implement company orders while in command of the *Tiger Bay* that he felt jeopardized the safety of ship and crew. He eventually left the command in protest.[20] Other captains report being dismissed for failing to carry out orders with which they disagreed.[21]

Not infrequently, a captain faces an intractable dilemma. The law usually requires that "no captain shall go to sea with a ship, unless the ship meets the requirements for the safety, health, and welfare of the crew" and the ship itself.[22] Before weighing anchor, the captain may be aware that there are deficiencies, some that are causing inconvenience, such as a broken boiler resulting in no hot water, and some that jeopardize safety, such as inoperable fire extinguishers, or lifeboats that do not launch. At what point does he decide to obey the law rather than company orders? He is caught between his responsibility to the shipowner and his legal obligations, which vary from country to country and from port to port.

The captain is also responsible for mountains of paperwork. Documents must be filed regularly with each port, with the shipowner, with the union, and sometimes with the registering country. John McPhee recalls that Captain Paul McHenry Washburn of the *Stella Lykes* waits until the roll of the ship knocks the pile of papers from his desk onto the deck. Surrounded by the papers, he then deals with them one by one nonstop until he clears the deck.[23]

Personnel issues on board are ultimately the captain's responsibility. Barnes tells of a captain whose health was jeopardized by the weight of this responsibility. As a youngster he had aspired to a maritime career and in the beginning had been full of enthusiasm, but after thirteen years at sea his enthusiasm had waned. One of his brothers, also a captain, had lost his life when his ship capsized, and after that he was very nervous about his own command. A series of unfortunate incidents increased his anxiety. His ship grounded once, and he barely escaped with his life. Another time his ship was stranded for forty-five days in the tropics. There was a serious equipment failure and he had all he could do to prevent a serious revolt among the crew.

His most vexing problem was maintaining crew discipline. His authority was constantly being tested.

> He described how difficult it was to make the crew members carry out their work. On one occasion the ratings claimed overtime wages for 100 hours per person to clean the water tanks. He was annoyed with their excessive demand. He gave all the concerned crew members a day off on a Sunday. With the help of two cadets he himself washed the tanks in four hours. Though he did it, he was apprehensive of reporting this incident of non-cooperative attitude of crew members to the office because he feared he would himself be reprimanded by the company for doing that job.[24]

On another occasion a crew member had a nervous breakdown and had to be hospitalized, leaving the rest of the crew unnerved, and still later a crew member on night duty was convinced that he had been beaten by a ghost. Thereafter, all the members of the crew refused night duty, because they were superstitious. During all of these incidents it was the captain who had to restore confidence. The burden of command had become very difficult. He was coping, but he was clearly in need of help.

The burdens of stress are frequently ignored by the agencies responsible for the management of the ship. Seafarers are often blamed for what goes wrong on board when they are but the victims of management that ignores stressful conditions that could be eliminated.

SEVEN
What Can Be Done?

BELIEVE I have made it clear that there is a great deal of suffering at sea. What I may not have made as clear is that there are many decent people working in the shipping industry, and many working seafarers get a fair deal from their employers. Throughout the world, there are shipowners, shipping companies, registries, and unions that take seriously their responsibility for the lives and welfare of the seafarers who work for them. One such company is the Zim Lines of Israel.

In the spring of 1981, the Zim Lines sent two personnel experts, called facilitators, to the *Vered* for five weeks to work with the crew to improve life on board. There were several positive results. A cultural affairs committee was developed to sponsor parties, quiz games were held that focused on the ship and its operation, and cultural events for the crew were planned. A procedure was instituted for introducing new employees, and study groups were organized, as well as a safety committee. The project was so successful that the Zim Lines sent teams of facilitators to all of the ships in its fleet.[1]

Companies like Zim have demonstrated what it means to take responsibility for the dignity of workers. There are others. Some shipping companies of Eastern Europe, realizing the deleterious effects of stress, place a doctor on board to plan cultural and sporting events and to deal with psychological problems. I have mentioned earlier in the book the *Bauchi* and its sister ships owned and operated by Torvald Klaveness & Co. There are many such enlightened ship operators with vessels in the liner and bulk trades.

There is also at least one well-organized and effective international ship registry, that of Liberia. Liberia has demonstrated that an international registry can function efficiently and humanely. In recent years, whenever the Center for Seafarers' Rights has contacted the Liberian ship registry on behalf of an individual seafarer or an entire crew, the international registry office, located in Reston, Virginia, has investigated the complaint. In 1989, we received an urgent call from seafarers in Piraeus, Greece, saying that the water on their ship, the *Ruby*, was severely rationed, linens had not been provided, the food was inadequate, and there were other problems. We were unable to reach a chaplain in Greece to verify the complaint, which is our normal practice, but we passed the complaint on to the Liberian registry nonetheless. The registry in turn contacted the owner, a well-known American company, which immediately sent one of its senior officers to Piraeus to investigate. He found that the situation was not as bad as the seafarers had claimed but that there were serious problems. If the Center for Seafarers' Rights had complained directly to the shipowner, the response might not have been so decisive. But the Liberian registry could bring the weight of its authority to bear on the problem and there was a positive outcome.

In many specific cases, maritime unions, despite their weaknesses, have helped seafarers achieve justice and given them hope. The International Transport Workers' Federation, for example, supports a network of "foc [flag-of-convenience] inspectors," many of whom have intervened on behalf of exploited seafarers and mistreated crew. A committed and concerned group, foc inspectors have gone out of their way in many situations to show their solidarity with unprotected workers. Again and again, chaplains have called on these inspectors to help seafarers in need. Rarely have the chaplains been disappointed.

The ITF has kept hope alive for decent wages and better working conditions. National union organizations are limited in structure and vision by national boundaries and loyalties and are impotent in bargaining with the international maritime industry. Only an international labor organization such as the ITF has the power to confront management in a truly international industry.

Seafarers have other advocates as well. In 1985, the Seamen's Church Institute created the Seafarers' Legal Services office, which offers free legal assistance to merchant seafarers who are unable to pay. Attorney Michael Steven Smith, a highly qualified legal aid attorney, served as director of that office for six years and he in turn organized a network of lawyers around the world who represent seafarers free of charge.

Support services for seafarers have been organized in several port cities: the Philippine Seamen's Assistance Program in Rotterdam, the Netherlands; the Centro de los Derechos del Marino in Barcelona, Spain; and the Maritime Education and Research Center in Manila, the Philippines. These volunteer centers are all involved in research, education, and advocacy.

Unfortunately, companies such as Zim Lines, registries such as Liberia's, and effective unions such as the ITF are the exceptions rather than the rule in today's maritime industry. In the rest of this chapter I will attempt to summarize why this is so and propose some specific reforms.

Clearly, the personnel policies in many shipping companies have seriously deteriorated. To understand why, one must first understand today's shipowners.[2] In the past, shipowners, whether gentlemen or rogues, were at least human beings with names, an office address, and a responsibility. Most were independent and conservative and eschewed any form of public meddling in the operation of their ships or fleets, but at least they were people to whom one could appeal. In our thinking, we still may have what has been called a "seductive image" of the shipowner. The image "is probably most associated in the popular mind with the Onasis-style Greek tycoon, building an ever-expanding empire of floating assets and untaxed income."[3]

Shipowning today is so capital-intensive and risky that not many individuals can afford to own a ship. Some captains dream of owning and operating their own ships, but usually the cost is so great and shipping so competitive that they do not succeed; invariably, the crew suffers in the process, as in the tragic case of the Galini.

In 1982, this thirty-two-year-old Honduran-flag vessel, a worn-out 5,150-ton ship, arrived in Venezuela, where it was abandoned by its owners. After two years of litigation, the Venezuelan court gave the ship to the captain, Anastasios Konstas, and six crew members in proportions equal to the amount the original owners owed them. The new owners gave a share to their lawyer and took on three Venezuelan partners, who financed repairs on the ship. There were now a total of eleven owners.

Konstas was thrilled to be an "owner" at last, but his delight soon turned to suffering. In twelve months he could find only two cargoes, and when the Galini arrived in New Orleans on September 20 to offload iron silicate, the U.S. Coast Guard detained it until repairs were made on the radar and gyrocompass. After two months of waiting for the repairs to be made and many months of not being paid, thirteen crew members put a lien on the ship to recover back wages. The four other members of the crew, who were part owners, opposed the lien; two of the thirteen were also owners but had to back out because they were in effect suing themselves. One of these thirteen was the new captain, Haralabos Karagianakis, who was suffering from diabetes and gangrene and wanted to be relieved of his duties and flown home to Greece.

By December, the ship had anchored in the Mississippi

River. There was enough food for only two more meals, according to Jack Booth of the Stella Maris Seamen's Center, and very little fuel. The ship was in danger of losing electricity for lights, refrigeration, and the distillation of water. Tensions were running high. Some of the crew wanted to drop the suit so the ship could sail to the Far East to be scrapped. Others feared that if they did they would never see their money. Konstas offered the seafarers three hundred dollars apiece if they would drop the suit, but, as a Chilean crew member, David Barrientos, said, "I am owed thousands; why should I accept three hundred dollars?"

A few weeks later tensions reached the breaking point, and Barrientos was killed in a fight with a Colombian first mate, Alvaro Martinez. Both had been drinking. The news stunned everyone; both men were known to be friendly, well educated, and easygoing. Barrientos had planned to settle with his wife and two young daughters in Toronto as soon as the dispute over the suit was ended.

Martinez was booked for murder but was released to the Stella Maris two weeks later. The judge decided that Martinez had acted in self-defense. He remained at the Stella Maris until February, when the ship was sold for $70,550—more than observers expected. After fees were paid, however, there was only enough to pay for the crew to be repatriated. There was nothing for salaries.

The *Galini* cost its owners all that they had and more and led to human and financial tragedy. Many of today's seafarers are likewise victimized by undercapitalized owners.[4]

Seafarers working on ships owned by large corporations are not necessarily better off than those that are owner operated. A corporation is often so complex and profit oriented that it does not respond to the needs of the workers. The case of the Liberian-registered *Pacific Charger* illustrates how complex ownership can be. When the *Pacific Charger* was stranded off New Zealand in May 1981, just a few weeks after it was launched, the court investigated to determine responsibility. The registered owners were Ocean Chargers

Company, Ltd., of Monrovia, Liberia, a subsidiary of Kansai Steamship Company of Japan. The first mortgage was held by Sumisho Lease Company. A second mortgage, held by Kurishimo Dockyard Company, was assigned to Sasebo Heavy Industries. Crusader Swire Container Services, Ltd., of London, an offshoot of Overseas Container Line, was in charge of operations. Documents were signed by John Swire and Sons (Japan) Ltd. Harmony Maritime, registered in Panama and located in Taipei, was the ship's manager. Harmony in turn subcontracted the responsibility of hiring officers to Union Maritime Company of Taiwan and of hiring ratings to the Ocean Services Company of Hong Kong through the Seamen's Control Division of the Rangoon, Burma, Marine Department. It is easy to see how the welfare of seafarers could get lost in this maze.

To reduce liability, most ships are "owned" by a separate, independent corporation, thereby hiding the true identity of the owner behind a legal veil. Day-to-day operation of the vessel is the responsibility of a managing company, which may be a totally separate contractor whose only goal is to operate profitably. It is not surprising that the quality of the workplace suffers when the primary decision makers are lawyers and financiers who make their decisions based on what will produce the maximum profits.

The relationship between shipowners and registries further protects the owners. Shipowners are clients of registries, and consequently all registries, including Liberia's, are reluctant to challenge the interests of shipowners.

In February 1989, when the Carnival Cruise Line's *Celebration* rammed and sank a Cuban fishing ship, resulting in the loss of several lives, the Liberian registry investigated. The full details of the investigation were not released, however. According to the registry, it did not want to limit the legal options of the operator and would not release its report until the litigation was completed. Whatever information may have been discovered in the investigation, which conceivably could have prevented further tragedies, was withheld to protect the interests of the owners.[5]

The Liberian registry office is a private business that operates under the cover of the nation of Liberia. The initiative to create the registry came from shipowning corporations that wanted to avoid taxes, labor unions, and, in some cases, safety standards required by the laws of the United States and other traditional maritime nations. Liberia was willing to cooperate with a program of ship registration. The arrangement that evolved benefits Liberia in that it receives income when a ship is registered with its office, and Liberian officials are able to participate in international maritime deliberations. At the same time, by being an independent corporation that has a contractual arrangement with Liberia, the registry remains immune from serious interference from Liberia and the uncertain politics of Liberia itself. When it is not clear which leader or party is in power, income from registration is held in escrow until the situation becomes more stable.[6] For the convenience of shipowners and other entrepreneurs, the Reston, Virginia, office creates "off-shore" corporations for any purpose, all ostensibly controlled by the laws of the sovereign state of Liberia. There is no doubt that the primary purpose of this enterprise is to serve the financial needs of its clients—shipowners and other entrepreneurs.

The ludicrous proliferation of ship registries has undermined the very concept of registration. At least five ships were reported to fly the flag of Belize when Belize had not yet established a ship registry office. These registrations were counterfeits. As long as the registration process continues on its present course, countless "bargain-basement" registries will continue to outdo one another in neglecting standards.

If flag states do not enforce standards, then port states must fill the vacuum. But does the industry want to yield total responsibility for enforcing standards to port states, many of which apply different standards and different enforcement procedures? A more desirable option would be to reform international registration policy. For the time being, however, a single international registry is a political impossibility. The sovereign states that currently register ships would not be willing to sacrifice the benefits they derive from the existing system. Many make substantial income, even charging as little as one dollar a ton. The Republic of Panama, for example, has 62,183,949 tons under its flag.

The freedom of shipowners to shift from one registry to another and from one labor-supplying country to another affects not only the seafarers on board ship but the effectiveness of union organizing. A healthy maritime industry requires an effective and democratic union to represent the welfare of seafarers, who are otherwise voiceless in their workplace.

The ITF has campaigned to eliminate flag-of-convenience registration altogether and to require that there be a genuine link between the shipowner and the country of registry. But this campaign has failed. The stated goal of the ITF continues to be the elimination of flag-of-convenience registries. This is an unrealistic goal in today's world, however, where half the ships are now flying flags of convenience. Meanwhile, the ITF continues to organize crews on flag-of-convenience vessels and by whatever means possible persists in its mission to eliminate the exploitation of the maritime worker. The ITF is one maritime organization that could truly represent today's maritime worker.

In addition to unions, church-sponsored agencies have advocated for seafarers for almost two centuries, but they are not always dependable. They have sometimes been so concerned about seafarers' spiritual salvation that they have neglected worldly protections. Archibald Mansfield, the director of the Seamen's Church Institute early in the twentieth century, had to persuade the church that advocacy was a legitimate ministry:

> The life of the sailor was of necessity a hard one, due to long voyages, often of several years' duration, the impossibility of

keeping fresh food on board, cramped quarters, and enormous dangers. . . . The social conscience was stirred, not by any means to the point of giving Jack a decent break on shipboard, but the necessity was felt of setting up provisions for saving his soul—to assure him of compensation in the next world. . . . I suppose as the shipping companies grew rich on his degradation and misery, the church opened wide her doors to offer consolation. . . . The three forces worked quietly side by side—the shipping company, the crimp, and the church, each attending to its own interests and not interfering with one another.[7]

Port chaplains around the world are effective in confronting violations and working for the basic human rights of seafarers. There is now a network of well-informed chaplains who will go into action when there is trouble on board. This is a new phenomenon in the maritime world. Port chaplains often meet resistance, however, from the boards of directors of the seamen's centers who employ them, and in many cases these boards are more sympathetic to shipowners than to seafarers. The boards are often self-perpetuating organizations made up primarily of established members of the community—people who can raise money but who do not necessarily empathize with today's seafarers. Chaplains, who are accountable to these boards, often must struggle for the right to act on behalf of seafarers in the political and economic sectors of society. Board members sometimes consider such action as beyond the legitimate function of the church. The tendency of the church to avoid conflict or deny conflicts that already exist further reduces effectiveness.

The following story from the annals of the Center for Seafarers' Rights illustrates the problem. The center—a program division of the Seamen's Church Institute of New York and New Jersey, a not-for-profit independent corporation—is ultimately accountable to an elected board of managers, which controls the budget. In January 1984, as director of the center, I organized a major international conference in Miami on the welfare of seafarers on cruise ships.

While our conference did not in any way condemn the

cruise ship industry as a whole, it presented evidence that living and working conditions on some cruise ships were abominable. At the conclusion of the conference, Bishop René Gracida, the Catholic bishop of Corpus Christi, Texas, who had been appointed by the Vatican to promote maritime ministry in the United States, proposed a boycott of any cruise ship company that continued to mistreat its crew. The attendees at the conference—one hundred people from the church, academia, and the unions of eighteen different countries—passed a resolution calling for the boycott, which was to be organized by the Center for Seafarers' Rights. Some of the union representatives present were hesitant, but otherwise the resolution met with great enthusiasm.

The next step was to develop the networks necessary to implement the boycott. A magazine for travel agents agreed to cooperate by reporting the boycott as a news event, and attorney James T. Lafferty was hired as the associate director of the Center for Seafarers' Rights to help implement it. As a social activist, Lafferty had represented labor causes in Detroit and was eminently qualified for his new job.

At the same time, the American maritime labor movement, stimulated by the Miami conference, renewed its efforts to organize seafarers on cruise ships registered in flag-of-convenience countries. Maritime unions had tried to organize these workers before, but the Supreme Court had ruled that the National Labor Relations Act did not protect flag-of-convenience seafarers on ships.[8] A seafarer who joined a union could be fired for doing so, and there was no government protection. Nonetheless, even without the protection of the National Labor Relations Act, hundreds of seafarers joined the newly formed International Maritime Union (IMU), and eventually a collective bargaining agreement was negotiated between the IMU and the cruise line that had been targeted for the boycott.

Not wanting to interfere with the IMU's organizing effort, the Center for Seafarers' Rights dropped its plan to stage a boycott. It had never been the center's intention to preempt the role of the unions in advocating for seafarers.

We encouraged the IMU in its organizing activities and helped organize some informational picketing of cruise ships. We also submitted testimony in a court case in New Orleans in which a seafarer claimed he was not being paid adequately according to the laws of Panama covering overtime. Members of the Board of Managers of the Seamen's Church Institute challenged these activities of the center. Some members also accused the center of being tools of the union movement. Ironically, it was also being attacked by the unions for being tools of the shipowners. More than once I was called to task by the unions for interfering with their work. The encouragement and gratitude we were receiving from seafarers all over the world was what kept us going.

I had first learned about social change as an active member of the Williamston, North Carolina, chapter of the Southern Christian Leadership Conference (SCLC). We believed that justice requires a change in laws and structures, not piecemeal consolation for those who are hurt. I had helped create the Massachusetts chapter of SCLC, which helped organize several boycotts of the Boston Public Schools, in an effort to overcome de facto racial segregation there. Subsequently, I was active in the National Welfare Rights Organization, which sought to reform America's welfare system. Whether I would be allowed to continue to practice my vocation of working for social change within the context of the institute became a serious question. Nonetheless, I considered myself fortunate to be working with a staff, directed by Jim Whittemore, that provided the climate in which I could take important steps toward achieving justice for seafarers.

Increasingly, I wondered, however, whether I could continue at the Seamen's Church Institute. I was being told that the mission of the center was to respond to those who were hurt by the injustices in the maritime industry but not to challenge the injustices themselves. It was not enough for me just to fish people out of the stream. It was necessary that I go upstream and see who was throwing them in and what could be done about it.

Clearly, larger problems remain that no one person or group, regardless of its valorous intentions, can tackle alone. These problems raise serious, controversial questions about our economic system.

There has been much praise recently for the benefits of the free market economy, but difficult questions remain about freedom for whom and to do what. The abuses and exploitation I have described occur within the free market economy. How free is it if it is controlled by only about two hundred large corporations, many of which are beyond the control of any sovereign nations? As we have seen, these corporations seem to have laws unto themselves.

In a recent case, the Center for Seafarers' Rights sought to use the laws of Ecuador to defend seafarers on an Ecuadorian ship that was owned and operated by a private Norwegian shipping company. The seafarers were clearly being exploited. We were told by government authorities in Ecuador that in view of the world economic situation, their government was unable to challenge the hegemony exercised by the shipping company over the sovereign state of Ecuador. Ecuador was an attractive country in which to invest because there was a supply of cheap labor, a powerless trade union organization, and ample tax concessions. Furthermore, it was easy to transfer profits back to Norway. In making itself attractive to foreign investors, Ecuador had also allowed the shipping company to dictate its national policy.

If profits, usually quick profits, are the primary goal of transnational corporations, they will inevitably be made at the expense of natural resources and working people. The exploitation of the work force in turn leads to the destabilization of international order.

The present economy, which gives free reign to transnational corporations, is not sacrosanct. It was created by human beings, and while it seems at times that the economy operates according to its own inexorable laws, it is possible to define new directions for economic institutions, including the shipping industry. Essential to this process is a commitment to the proposition that all human enterprises must be measured by their effect on the people who participate in them.

Following these broad guidelines, I would like to propose some reforms that would greatly improve the life of seafarers. Some companies and governments have already adopted some of these policies.

1. Worker associations are essential. Every worker should be free to belong to a legitimate association that gives voice to his or her concerns. An individual worker is at a total disadvantage in trying to negotiate fair terms with a corporation. Only in solidarity with other workers can he or she hope to achieve fair terms. Several nations have acknowledged the right of seafarers to organize and to belong to unions—a right that is affirmed by ILO Conventions No. 87 and 98. Few nations, however, encourage their workers to participate actively in workers' associations. A collective bargaining process is essential to a just workplace, especially in an industry that is so impersonal. To quote from an adaptation of Pope John Paul II's encyclical *On Human Work*, "History has taught us that unions are indispensible for the protection of rights."[9]

2. Workers need to have permanent contracts providing them with the pension and social security benefits that are enjoyed by shore-based workers. Labor-supplying countries should work toward such requirements.

3. The length of time at sea should be reduced to about two months on and two months off so that seafarers can participate in the life of the society, the community, and the family. When Western unions were strong, they were working toward such a goal.

4. The policy of "fixed overtime" should be outlawed and an ILO convention passed to that effect. A maximum number

of hours of overtime per week has to be established and, except in life-threatening emergencies, followed. Records need to be kept of actual overtime hours worked and seafarers paid accordingly.

5. Shipowners should provide for worker participation in the decisions that affect seafarers' lives. Workers need to have information and some control over the recruiting process and to participate in the decision-making process on board ship. Regular meetings of the crew in which details of the voyage as well as interpersonal issues are discussed would help seafarers feel that they are not just replaceable parts of a machine.

6. Seafarers should be given greater opportunity to participate in the corporate policies of their employers. Several arrangements exist in other industries: profit sharing, stock-holding options, and cooperative ownership.[10]

7. Registering countries should not protect the identity of phantom owners. They should clearly identify a responsible decision maker, for what chance does the seafarer have of achieving justice when the employer remains anonymous and unavailable?

Ultimately, basic change can come only from seafarers themselves. Most of these suggested reforms require a re-balance of power. History shows that those in positions of power do not yield their power voluntarily. It is only as seafarers realize their own strength that they will be able to claim authority over their own lives.

Ironically, in the eighteenth century piracy represented an attempt on the part of seafarers to overcome some of the most obvious abuses of shipboard life. One such abuse was the denial of any participation in the decision-making process. It is common knowledge that merchant seafarers turned to piracy so they could plunder and enrich themselves. What is less well known is that piracy was a deliberate and calculated rebellion against the oppressive and hierarchical structure of cargo ships at the time. Seafarers often quit legitimate seafaring jobs and joined pirate ships to protest their inhumane treatment. They sometimes delighted in the vengeful execution of a captured captain who was known for mistreating workers, but they would also protect the life of a captain whose crew attested to his justice as a leader.

In their heyday, from 1716 to 1726, pirates were organized in an egalitarian society that embodied some of the principles of social justice that they had been denied on commercial ships. Marcus Rediker notes that a "striking uniformity of rules and customs prevailed aboard pirate ships, each of which functioned under the terms of written articles, a compact drawn up at the beginning of a voyage or upon election of a new captain, and agreed to by the crew. By these articles crews allocated authority, distributed plunder and enforced discipline."[11]

Seafaring is a proud profession with a glorious tradition. Some of the most sublime literature has been inspired by life at sea. The unpredictable oceans and the dauntless courage of those who cross them are sources of continuous inspiration and excitement. It is neither right nor necessary that any seafarer today should have to work under conditions reminiscent of those in the days when pirates roamed the seas.

NOTES

PREFACE

1. *Bermuda Royal Gazette*, Feb. 26, 1985. I am grateful to Captain Sir David Tibbetts and to Ron Ross for information about the *Frusa*.
2. Dana, Jr., *Two Years before the Mast*, 6.

INTRODUCTION

1. In contrast, maritime policy makers have written a great deal about employment practices in the industry, particularly with regard to methods to improve efficiency and their implications for the size of crews. For a sample of the writing by academics and practitioners, see Donn, *Foreign Competition* and *Concession Bargaining*; National Research Council, *Effective Manning*; and Northrup and Rowan, *The International Transport Workers' Federation and Flag of Convenience Shipping*.
2. Donn and Karper, "Changing Product Markets," 86.
3. See Donn, *Foreign Competition*, for a detailed discussion of these issues as they relate to the U.S.-flag fleet. One of the principal reasons for smaller crews is that changes in propulsion systems during the 1970s and 1980s enabled many tasks that were previously done manually to be mechanized and computerized.
4. Kilgour, *The United States' Merchant Marine*, 6.
5. See Carlisle, *Sovereignty for Sale*, for a detailed discussion of the history of open registries.
6. Donn, *Flag of Convenience Registry*, 140.
7. Ibid., 141.
8. Ibid., 140.
9. See Northrup and Rowan, *The International Transport Workers' Federation*, for a detailed and highly skeptical account of this campaign.
10. See Donn and Phelan, "Australian Maritime Unions," for an account of the Australian component of the ITF flag of convenience campaign.
11. In 1987, for example, the ILO raised the recommended monthly wage for seafarers from $276 to $286 (Donn, *Flag of Convenience Registry*, 140). This is less than half the rate in the standard ITF contract at the time. See Argiroffo, "Flags of Convenience and Substandard Vessels," for a discussion of the ILO's approach to this problem.
12. Determining ownership of a flag-of-convenience vessel is often not a simple task. Typically, the vessel must be nominally owned by a company in the flag state, but often the owner is just a paper corporation set up for the purpose of purchasing a ship. Finding the ultimate owner may require a search through a maze of paper corporations.

148

CHAPTER 1. THE SEA AS A WORKPLACE

1. Many of these books are listed in the references.
2. Dana, Jr., *Two Years before the Mast*, 46.
3. Ibid., 101.
4. Samuels, *From the Fo'c'sle to the Cabin*, 141.
5. Ibid., 146.
6. To their credit, the Liberian registry, being the last registry of record, undertook a thorough investigation of this case and barred the owner, Aristotle Voulgaris, from ever registering his ships in Liberia again. Subsequently, after a similar incident in Trinidad, Voulgaris was temporarily barred from registering in Panama. In 1988, however, a close associate of Voulgaris, who was identified in the Liberian investigation as a partner, imported a Burmese crew to the *Lady V*, registered in Panama, for the purpose of repairing old tonnage.
7. Some cruise lines put considerable pressure on passengers to tip their employees—thus increasing the cost of the cruise by seventy to one hundred dollars per week. When passengers on these ships do not tip waiters, stewards, busboys, and so on, they deprive them of up to 90 percent of their expected salary. The Holland American Line has now abolished the tipping system, acknowledging its injustices. Wade, "American Pie," 12.
8. "Because the harbor was not suitable to winter in, the majority advised to put to sea from there." Acts 27:12.
9. Laws of Oleron, art. II, page 1171, quoted in thirty federal cases.

CHAPTER 2. GETTING A JOB

1. Lloyd, *British Seaman*, 58.
2. Rediker, *Between the Devil and the Deep Blue Sea*, 81ff.
3. Lloyd, *British Seaman*, 148.
4. See Fingard, *Jack in Port*.
5. Standard, *Merchant Seamen*, 67ff.
6. Speech delivered by President Ferdinand E. Marcos at the First National Congress on Overseas Employment, July 20, 1982, Manila, and quoted in Catholic Institute for International Relations, *The Labour Trade*, 120.
7. Asia-Pacific Mission for Migrant Filipinos, *Proceedings of the Fourth Regional Conference*, 112. The actual amount of money remitted to the Philippines may be far higher than the Central Bank figures. According to the *Manila Sunday Times* of July 9, 1989, "Filipinos working overseas sent home an estimate of US$2.5 billion last year. Central Bank records show that Filipinos abroad remitted only US$857 million through the banking system, the others relying on couriers and carrier firms. POEA chief, Tomas Achacoso, said that the International Labor Organization has estimated that Filipino overseas workers actually remitted US$2.5 billion." In 1990 José Sarmiento, POEA chief, estimated remittances are as high as $4 billion.

8. Petrucelli, "The Price of Fish," 6.
9. Guest, "Industry Ponders How to Raise Standards," 81.

CHAPTER 3. EMPLOYMENT INJUSTICES

1. Ancient maritime tradition regards the written contract between the master and the seafarer as essential to the ship's operation. As early as 1729 the statutes of England required under penalty that no master bound on a foreign voyage could carry any seaman or mariner to sea without first reaching an agreement with such seaman. The agreement had to be in writing and signed by the seaman (Act 2, George II, chap. 36, ## 1, 2).

   U.S. law incorporates ancient maritime practice. Several of the following citations expand on the history of the agreement. The agreement, called "Shipping Articles" or "Articles of Agreement," is the seafarer's contract and is an agreement originally between the master and the seafarer (*Stevens v. Seacoast Co., Inc.*, 414F.2d, 1032, 1969 AMC 1911 (1969 CA5 Miss.). Both must sign. But as Justice Joseph Story has written, "The contract created by the shipping articles is not, by the maritime law, a contract exclusively between the existing master and the seamen for the voyage. It is rather a contract between the seamen and the owner through the instrumentality of the master, as agent of the owner. . . . For the performance of the contract, however, the seamen have the security of the master and the owner and also of the ship itself by a lien thereon for their wages" (*U.S. v. Haines*, F Cas No 15275 (1829 D.C. Mass.)).

   If the contract is not in writing, then the seafarer is not bound by it, and, should a dispute arise, his testimony under oath is to be determinative: "Title Fourth of the Marine Ordinances of Louis XIV provided as follows: all agreements between masters and their seamen shall be reduced into a writing . . . ; if otherwise, the seamen's oath shall be believed" (*Smith v. Chase*, F Cas No 13023 (1876 D.C. Me.)), cited in Norris, *The Law of Seamen*, 178.

2. The articles must be signed before the vessel proceeds to sea. "Whenever a seaman is shipped, he is entitled to know at once the terms of his engagement, that he may exercise his option of leaving the vessel before she weighs anchor" (F Cas No 13880 (1878 D.C. Mich.)).

3. The 1983 bilateral agreement law is Greek law 1376. It may be in conflict with Article 22 of the Greek constitution, which guarantees equal pay for equal work, and it appears to be in conflict with Article 83 of the Greek maritime code, which says all seafarers on Greek registered ships should be paid according to Greek union wages. Nevertheless, Greek court decision 1588 affirmed the constitutionality of law 1376.

4. Smith, "Trends and Patterns in Human Rights Violations," 76.

5. In an agreement requiring "fixed" overtime, the seafarer is entitled to the same total overtime regardless of the number of overtime hours he works. Such contracts are obviously weighted against the

seafarer in that overtime pay can be reduced when the seafarers work only a few hours of overtime but is not increased when they work extra-long hours.

6. Smith, "Trends and Patterns Human Rights Violations," 79.
7. The Jones Act (Merchant Marine Act of 1920) allows any seafarer to seek compensation for personal injury by claiming that a breach of the "warranty of seaworthiness," implied in his contract, caused his illness or injury. For a U.S. federal court to take jurisdiction in such a case, at least some of the following points of contact between the vessel and the U.S. have to be weighed: the place where the injury took place, the country of registry, the nationality or home of the injured or sick seafarer, the nationality or home or place of business of the employer, the place where the contract was signed, and the ease with which a seafarer could use the court of another country.
8. Radiotelevisione Italiana, *Ships to Sink*, 10.
9. Ibid., 44.
10. Scarrot, "Floating Coffins," 31.
11. The Standards of Training, Certification and Watchkeeping Convention (STCW) of the International Maritime Organization, a United Nations–related agency, prescribes the minimum qualifications for officers in nautical, engineering, and radio departments. Each ratifying country writes its own enabling legislation, which determines enforcement procedures and penalties.
12. Jungblut, "Need a License?" 38.
13. Smith, "Trends and Patterns in Human Rights Violations," 82. The archives of the Seamen's Church Institute record an incident in which a captain, seeing how unsafe a ship was, left the ship and took the train from Maine to New York rather than face the dangers that the crew was forced to endure.
14. Ibid., 80.
15. *La Voz*, June 7, 1984, 1.

CHAPTER 4. UNIONS—EAST AND WEST
1. Morison, *Maritime History of Massachusetts*, 352.
2. Archives of the Seamen's Church Institute, New York.
3. Morison, *Maritime History of Massachusetts*, 354.
4. Barnes, *Evolution and Scope of Mercantile Marine Laws*, 41.
5. Lane, *Grey Dawn Breaking*, 17.
6. Brooks, ed., Seafarers in the ASEAN Region, 102.
7. Nelson, *Workers on the Waterfront*, 33.
8. Rediker, *Between the Devil and the Deep Blue Sea*, 205. According to C. R. Dobson, spontaneous strikes for better wages were recorded as early as 1739. See Dobson, *Master and Journeymen*.
9. Standard, *Merchant Seamen*, 15.
10. Albrecht, *International Seamen's Union of America*, 4.
11. Standard, *Merchant Seamen*, 189.
12. See Marsh, *A History of the National Union of Seamen*, chaps. 4, 15.
13. Nelson, *Workers on the Waterfront*, 48.

14. Marsh, *National Union of Seamen*, chap. 3, ms. p. 17.
15. Axtell, *Merchant Seamen's Law*, 6. In writing to seafarers about the virtues of the new law, Furuseth implied that freedom to jump ship was now one of the great freedoms guaranteed under the American flag. At sea, duty is required, but "in a safe harbor you are under the law of freedom."
16. See McPhee, *Looking for a Ship*.
17. Lane, *Grey Dawn Breaking*, 182.
18. Nelson, *Workers on the Waterfront*, 273.
19. See Golding, *ITF*.
20. Northrup and Rowan, *International Transport Workers' Federation and Flag of Convenience Shipping*, 43.
21. A portion of the assets of the Seafarers' International Welfare Assistance and Protection Fund are contributed each year to a charitable trust, the ITF Seafarers' Trust, with assets in 1989 of $40 million. From this trust up to $4 million has been contributed annually to seafarers' centers around the world for vans, building needs, phone systems, and other capital expenses.
22. Each Third World ITF affiliate has its own story. The Indonesian Seafarers' Union (Kesatuan Pelaut Indonesia, or ISU) joined ITF in April 1981 because an Indonesian-owned ship registered in Liberia was being held up by a dock workers' strike organized by the ITF. The Indonesian government asked the union to negotiate with the ITF for the release of the vessel, but the ITF refused to negotiate unless the ISU would join as an affiliate. The ISU joined, and the strike was settled. At that time there were 73,000 registered seafarers in Indonesia, of whom 36,000 were at work. As of August 1991, however, the ITF still had not recognized the collective bargaining agreements of the ISU and therefore had not issued blue cards to ships with a contract with the union. See Brooks, ed., *Seafarers in the ASEAN Region*, 144.
23. Seafarers' Accreditation Division, Philippines Overseas Employment Administration, 1988.
24. See Green, *Against the Tide*, the story of corruption in maritime unions in Canada.

CHAPTER 5. MARITIME LAW AND
THE PROTECTION OF SEAFARERS

1. This law was published in Lübeck in 1597.
2. Chap. 16, art. 11, Consulado del Mar, Barcelona (1494).
3. 18 U.S. (5 Wheat.), 417.
4. *Regina v. Anderson*, 11 Cox's Criminal Cases, 198.
5. *New York Newsday*, Oct. 18, 1988, 4.
6. Lloyd's Register, *Statistical Tables*, shows the relative size of various flag-of-convenience fleets.
7. In the case of *Vinuela v. SS Britanis* (SDNY 1986) 647 F. Supp. 1139, the expert explained that judicial precedents are not used in subsequent decisions in Panama and that the Ministry of Labor and

Social Welfare has a judicial function to interpret the law. In this case, it found certain provisions of the law inapplicable (e.g., the requirement for overtime pay, the requirement of "thirteenth month" social security pay, the requirement for a written contract). In the case of *Daniel Henry et al. v. the SS Bermuda Star* (Civil Action No. 85–5307, Sec. A, District Court, Louisiana), the expert underlined that the code must be flexible in order to serve the needs of the many different nationalities flying the Panamanian flag and that the law is open to local interpretation. "The phraseology of the [Labor] Code is not very uniform as it should be, but these articles provide for the specific and preferential application of the special provisions, and authorize the application of certain general norms of the Code. Frequent reference is made to international maritime usages and customs, which can be applied when convenient." He admitted to a "notorious lack of accuracy of the terminology of the code": "What the Panama labor law has wanted to do is guarantee both the seamen as well as the owner the application of practices, usages to which they both were accustomed and which are not equal all over the world but, rather, which vary in various parts of the world. . . . International maritime usages have priority over the general norms of the Labor Code."

8. According to 46 U.S.C. 10313.
9. 120 U.S. 1 11–12 (1887).
10. The United States can also become involved on purely humanitarian grounds. In 1790, in the case of *Weiberg v. the St. Oloff*, treaty stipulations gave the Swedish consul exclusive jurisdiction in a matter involving a Swedish seafarer on a Swedish-owned, Swedish-flag ship. Yet the U.S. court took jurisdiction when the Swedish captain put Weiberg in irons in retaliation for his bringing suit against the vessel. "Under the circumstances, the court took jurisdiction of the matter on humanitarian ground." (Norris, *Law of Seamen*, 114.) The court has complete discretion whether or not to take jurisdiction.
11. Minimum Age Convention, 1973 (No. 138) or Minimum Age (Sea) Convention (Revised), 1936 (No. 58), or Minimum Age (Sea) Convention, 1920 (No. 7); Shipowners' Liability (Sick and Injured Seamen) Convention, 1936 (No. 56) or Medical Care and Sickness Benefits Convention, 1969 (No. 130); Medical Examination (Seafarers) Convention 1946 (No. 73); Prevention of Accidents (Seafarers) Convention, 1970 (No. 134), Articles 4 and 7; Accommodation of Crews Convention (Revised), 1949 (No. 92); Food and Catering (Ships' Crews) Convention, 1946 (No. 68) (Article 5); Officers' Competency Certificates Convention, 1936 (No. 53) (Articles 3 and 4); Seamen's Article of Agreement Convention, 1926 (No. 22); Repatriation of Seamen Convention, 1926 No. 23); Freedom of Association and Protection of the Right to Organize Convention, 1948 (No. 87); and Right to Organize and Collective Bargaining Convention, 1949 (No. 98).
12. International Convention on Load Lines, 1966; International Con-

vention for Safety of Life at Sea, 1974; Protocol of 1978 relating to the International Convention for the Safety of Life at Sea, 1974; International Convention for the Prevention of Pollution from Ships, 1973, as modified by the Protocol of 1978 relating thereto; International Convention on Standards of Training, Certification and Watchkeeping for Seafarers, 1978; The Convention on the International Regulations for Preventing Collisions at Sea, 1972; and ILO Convention No. 147 (The Minimum Standards Conventions).

13. Memorandum of Understanding, sect. 3.2.

14. Herman Melville, *Moby Dick*, chap. 123.

15. See UNCTAD Secretariat, *Review and Analysis of Possible Measures to Minimize the Occurence of Maritime Fraud and Piracy*. UNCTAD has identified six major categories of fraud: documentary, charter party, marine insurance, deviation, miscellaneous, and piracy.

In 1981, an independent agency, the International Maritime Bureau, was established to combat maritime fraud. In its first decade, the IMB reported a continued increase in maritime fraud.

16. Stowell in the cases of *Juliana* (1822) and *Minerva* (1835) and Story in *Hardin v. Gordon* (1823) and *Brown v. Lull* (1936).

17. 4 F Cas Pag 409. Cf. Minerva 1 Gaff. 354; 166 E.R. 123: "These men who are the favorites of the law, on account of their imbecility, and placed particularly under its protection, may be made the victims of their own ignorance and simplicity. . . . To those who are acquainted with this court, it can be no secret how deeply some of these are affected with surprise and concern, when they find that they have ever executed any engagement drawing after it consequences so disastrous. . . . On the one side are gentlemen possessed of wealth and intent. . . . On the other side is a set of men generally ignorant and illiterate, notoriously and proverbially reckless and improvident."

18. Barnes, *Evolution and Scope of Mercantile Marine Laws Relating to Seamen in India*, 29.

19. *Robertson v. Baldwin*, 165 U.S. 275 (1897).

20. Borgese, *The Future of the Oceans*, 132.

CHAPTER 6. THE STRESSES OF SEAFARING

1. See Aubert, *The Hidden Society*. The concept was originally described by Erving Goffman in *Asylums: Essays on the Social Situation of Mental Patients and Other Inmates (1962)*.

2. An important exception is Barnes, *Mental Health of Officer Personnel in the Indian Merchant Marine*, based on a survey of personnel in the merchant marine in India.

3. The Mahant Hungarian Shipping Company, Ltd., developed an extensive battery of psychological tests to discover "the individuals with characteristics of personality, by the existence of which they are predestined to a successful seagoing career." Boehm, *International Workshop on Human Relations on Board*, 62.

4. According to a recent study conducted by Manolo Abella, former head of the Republic of the Philippines' Ministry of Labor's Institute of Labor and Manpower Studies, 32 percent of Filipino seafarers have a college degree. "Over half of the seamen (53.6 percent) completed high school and among them, nine out of ten went to college." Of Filipino deck officers, 72.9 percent have completed high school, and 59.6 percent have completed college; 97.9 percent of engine officers completed high school, and 87.5 percent have a college degree. Talampas, "Seafarer Intellectuals," 3.

5. Barnes, *Mental Health*, 117.

6. *Korea Maritime*, Sept.–Oct. 1988.

7. Barnes, *Mental Health*, 123.

8. See Leo Barnes, *Evolution and Scope of Mercantile Marine Laws Relating to Seamen in India*, 247.

9. The Philippine government's justification for the overseas workers program is that the money earned overseas, most of which is sent back home as family remittances, is invested in the Philippines. The policy assumes that increased spending in the local economy will generate demand for local products, thereby encouraging the growth of local trade, and in time increase the country's productive capacity and gross national product. The De la Salle study on the families of migrant workers indicates, however, that very few households use remittances to make productive investments. In order of priority, remittances are spent on basic necessities, debt repayment, education of children, housing needs, and savings. Only 4 percent of the workers were able to start their own businesses as a result of their overseas work. Most of the money simply went for consumer goods. One survey shows that 50 percent of the families receiving money from a worker abroad still run out of money before the next check comes. Go, Postrado, and Ramos-Jimenez, *The Effect of International Contract Labor*, 83.

10. Total loss statistics compiled from Lloyd's Register, *Statistical Tables*.

YEAR	NUMBER OF VESSELS
1978	473
1979	465
1980	387
1981	359
1982	402
1983	340
1984	327
1985	307
1986	265
1987	219
1988	231
1989	211

11. *Boboricken v. United States*, 76 F. Supp. 70, 1948 AMC 711 (1947, D.C. Wash).
12. Sherar, *Shipping Out*, 24.
13. Barnes, *Mental Health*, 148ff. Research on Western seafarers shows that they suffer many of the same stress-related illnesses.
14. Ibid., 193.
15. *Manila Daily Globe*, Sept. 3, 1988, 2.
16. See Brooks, ed., *Seafarers in the ASEAN Region*.
17. Barnes, *Mental Health*, 144, 156, 121. A captain one hundred years ago warned young people against a seagoing career: "I would not commit my memories to paper if I felt they would in the slightest tend to induce a boy to become a sailor. The rough experience I have gone through, few could live to endure." Samuels, *From the Fo'c'sle to the Cabin*, 3.
18. Private correspondence.
19. Grey, "Lookout," May 1990, 4.
20. Cheek, *Legacies of Peril*.
21. Nautical Institute, "Safety and Employment—Are They Linked?" 3.
22. This particular formulation is taken from the Indonesian Maritime Law, title 6, chap. 32. It is typical of most maritime laws regarding the captain's responsibility for safety.
23. McPhee, *Looking for a Ship*, 126.
24. Barnes, *Mental Health*, 158.

CHAPTER 7. WHAT CAN BE DONE?

1. Shafran, "The 'Vered'-Project," quoted in Boehm, *International Workshop,* 95ff.
2. See Smith, "Trends and Patterns in Human Rights Violations," 60. Captain Smith has identified seven types of ownership. Among these are ships owned by national shipping corporations that register the ship and employ the crew from the same country, and ships owned by international corporations, perhaps a bank or a pension fund, and registered and crewed according to market conditions. According to Smith, "As the link between ownership and crew/flag nationality becomes more tenuous, the more agencies intervene, the scope for sources of human rights abuse multiplies."
3. Davis, "How Should Britain Maintain Its Maritime Industries?" 77.
4. "What is wrong with shipping today is that it is far too like shipping of yesterday. Aging tonnage, casual labor, the use of managing agents, the cutting of margins to the bone, exploitation of the permanent state of conflict between the crew and owner by various troublemakers ashore and afloat. Goodness, you can pull out any of these hundred year old bound volumes that surround me as I write and find this scenario exactly.

"I suppose you really cannot blame under-capitalized owners who try and do things on the cheap with old bangers that ought to be hurried into demolition yards, if the system lets them get away with it. You cannot single out these people as criminals merely for operating their ships with the cheapest labor possible, any more than the old British tramp owner was criminal for taking advantage of a vast pool of distressed unemployed labor. It's the system that is wrong. By tightening up on standards, by insisting on properly trained crews on the best possible labor agreements, by strictly adhering to inspection procedures, we shall undoubtedly be increasing the cost of operating ships. But I suggest that the owners who will be shaken out of the industry by tightening of standards ought to be out of it. Meanwhile medieval attitudes toward labor, the justification of cheapness as a means to an end serves merely to perpetuate the problem." Grey, "Lookout," Feb. 1988, 2).

5. The Liberian registry defends its action by refering to IMO/SOLAS, chap. I, pt. C, reg. 21, which says that a registry's investigation shall not "in any manner fix or imply responsibility upon any ship or person." Reference is also made to a high court injunction in England that prohibited the Department of Transportation from publishing a casualty report of the *Zulfikar* accident in July 1991.

6. The Panamanian registry enjoys no such protection. The registry suffered serious losses when, in the fall of 1989, the United States initiated economic sanctions against the Noriega regime.

7. Mansfield, unpublished autobiography, 36ff.

8. In 1959, the National Maritime Union and the Seafarers International Union overcame their rivalry long enough to establish the International Maritime Workers Union, which for four years recruited foreign seafarers working on American-owned Panamanian, Liberian, and Honduran ships. Its success depended ultimately on whether it was protected by the National Labor Relations Act. When the U.S. Supreme Court ruled in February 1963 that it was not, the union folded. See Carlisle, *Sovereignty for Sale*, 165.

9. Concerned Seamen of the Philippines, *What the Church Says*, 15.

10. Ibid., 9: "The human rights of workers may be better protected when there is joint ownership of the means of work, and sharing by the workers in the management and/or profits. As the age of colonization and territorial possession is over, everyone must recognize the change in economic structures. . . . It is the people who must own the means of production, in order to ensure that everybody is fully entitled to consider themselves a part owner of the great workbench at which they are working with everyone else. As far as possible, labor should be the owner of capital. This could happen in a variety of decentralized structures in a society in which communities work for the common good—in which each member of the body would be looked upon and treated as persons and encouraged to take an active part in the life of the body. It is not enough just to get paid for the work you do. Human dignity requires

that in some way you know you are working for the common good, and in this sense, working for yourself. It is not enough to just be a cog in a wheel that is controlled by a centralized bureaucracy."

11.   Rediker, *Betwen the Devil and the Deep Blue Sea*, 261.

REFERENCES

ADAM, PAUL, ed. *Seamen in Society*. Bucharest: Commission Internationale d'Histoire Maritime, 1980.

ALBRECHT, ARTHUR EMIL. *International Seamen's Union of America: A Study of its History and Problems*. U.S. Bureau of Labor Statistics Miscellaneous Series no. 342. Washington, D.C.: Government Printing Office, 1923.

ALVAREZ, A. *Offshore: A North Sea Journey*. London: Hodder and Stoughton, 1986.

AOKI, SHUJI. "Review of the Occupation of Seamen in Japan." *Maritime Policy and Management* 7, no. 4 (1980).

APOSTLESHIP OF THE SEA. *Report of the Accra Meeting of the Apostleship of the Sea*. Vatican City: Pontifical Commission for Migration and Tourism, 1987.

ARGIROFFO, ENRICO. "Flags of Convenience and Substandard Vessels: A Review of the ILO's Approach." *International Labor Review* 113, no. 11 (November 1974).

————. "Recruitment of Seamen in Asia." *International Labor Review* 95 (March 1967).

ASIA-PACIFIC MISSION FOR MIGRANT FILIPINOS. *Proceedings of the Fourth Regional Conference of the Overseas Filipinos in Asia and the Pacific*. Hong Kong: Asia-Pacific Mission for Migrant Filipinos, 1990.

AUBERT, VILHELM. *The Hidden Society*. Totowa, N.J.: Bedminster Press, 1965.

AUBERT, VILHELM, and ODDVAR ARNER. *The Social System of the Ship*. Oslo: Institute for Social Research, 1962.

AUERBACH, JEROLD S. *Labor and Liberty: The La Follette Committee and the New Deal*. New York: Bobbs, Merrill, 1966.

————. "Progressives at Sea: The La Follette Act of 1915." *Labor History* 2 (1961).

AXTELL, SILAS B. *Merchant Seamen's Law*. New York: Consumers' Book Cooperative, 1943.

————. *Rights and Duties of Merchant Seamen*. New York: Merchant Seamen Publishing, 1920.

————. *A Symposium on Andrew Furuseth*. New Bedford, Mass.: Darwin Press, 1948.

BALL, JOSEPH H. *The Government-Subsidized Union Monopoly: A Study of Labor Practice in the Shipping Industry*. Washington, D.C.: Labor Policy Association, 1966.

BARNES, BLANCHE I. *Mental Health of Officer Personnel in the Indian Merchant Marine*. London: International Transport Workers' Federation, 1989.

BARNES, LEO. *Evolution and Scope of Mercantile Marine Laws Relating to Seamen in India*. New Dehli: Maritime Law Association, 1983.

BENFORD, HARRY. "Reduced Manning Poses Challenges for Managers." *Fairplay International Shipping Weekly*, Jan. 3, 1985.

BENSON, H. W. "Democracy and Union Conglomerates: A Report on Recent Trends in the NMU." *Dissent* 20 (1973).

BERNARD, H. RUSSELL. "On the Social Structure of an Ocean-Going Research Vessel and Other Important Things." *Social Science Research* 2 (1973).

BOCZEK, BOLESLAW ADAM. *Flags of Convenience: An International Legal Study*. Cambridge: Harvard University Press, 1962.

BOEHM, HELMUTH, ed. *International Workshop on Human Relationships on Board*. Bremen: Hochschule für Nautik, 1982.

———. "Isolation of Operators as a Consequence of Automation." In *Proceedings of a Workshop, Medical and Public Health Research Programme of the Commission of European Communities*. Bremen: Hochschule für Nautik, 1986.

BORGESE, ELISABETH MANN. *The Future of the Oceans*. Montreal: Harvest House, 1986.

BOURDET-PLEVILLE, MICHEL. *Justice in Chains: From the Galleys to Devil's Island*. London: Robert Hale, 1960.

BOYER, RICHARD. *The Dark Ship*. Boston: Little, Brown, 1947.

BROOKS, MARY R., ed. *Seafarers in the ASEAN Region*. Singapore: Institute of South East Asia Studies, 1989.

CADWALLDER, J. J. "Discipline in British Ships." *Journal of Maritime Law and Commerce* 2, no. 1 (1970).

CARLISLE, RODNEY P. *Sovereignty for Sale*. Annapolis, Md.: Naval Institute Press, 1981.

CATHOLIC INSTITUTE FOR INTERNATIONAL RELATIONS. *The Labour Trade: Filipino Migrant Workers around the World*. London: Catholic Institute for International Relations, 1987.

CHAPMAN, PAUL K. "Cruelty to Seamen: Young Richard Henry Dana Challenges Justice Joseph Story." *Log* 38, no. 2 (1986).

CHEEK, PHILIP MORGAN. *Legacies of Peril*. London: Book Guild, 1986.

CLARK, WILLIAM H. *Ships and Sailors: The Story of Our Merchant Marine*. Boston: Page, 1938.

CONCERNED SEAMEN OF THE PHILIPPINES. *What the Church Says to Merchant Seamen: An Adaptation of Paul John Paul II's Encyclical on Human Work*. Manila: Concerned Seamen of the Philippines, 1987.

COURSE, A. G. *The Deep Sea Tramp*. Barre, Mass.: Barre Publishing, 1963.

———. *The Merchant Navy: A Social History*. London: F. Fuller, 1963.

COWAN, EDWARD. *Oil and Water: The Torrey Canyon Disaster*. New York: J. B. Lippincott, 1968.

DANA, RICHARD HENRY, JR. *Two Years before the Mast*. 1840. Reprint. New York: P. F. Collier & Son, 1937.

DAVIS, J. G. "How Should Britain Maintain Its Maritime Industries?" *Seafarer*, Summer 1988.

DAVIS, RALPH. *The Rise of the English Shipping Industry in the Seventeenth and Eighteenth Centuries*. London: Macmillan, 1962.

DILLON, R. N. *Shanghaiing Days*. New York: Coward McCann, 1961.

DOBSON, C. R. *Masters and Journeymen*. London: Croom Helm, 1980.

DONN, CLIFFORD B. *Concession Bargaining in the Ocean-Going Maritime Industry*. Syracuse, N.Y.: LeMoyne College Institute of Industrial Relations, 1987.

———. *Flag of Convenience Registry and Industrial Relations: The Internationalization of National Flag Fleets*. Syracuse, N.Y.: LeMoyne College Institute of Industrial Relations, 1988.

———. *Foreign Competition, Technological Change and the Decline in Maritime Employment*. Syracuse, N.Y.: LeMoyne College Institute of Industrial Relations, 1987.

DONN, CLIFFORD B., and MARK D. KARPER, "Changing Product Markets and the New Industrial Relations in the USA." *Bulletin of Comparative Labor Relations* 20 (1990).

DONN, CLIFFORD B., RICHARD MORRIS, and G. PHELAN. *Reforms of Work Practices and Industrial Relations Procedures in the Maritime Industry: An Australia–United States Comparison*. Syracuse, N.Y.: LeMoyne College Institute of Industrial Relations, 1990.

DONN, CLIFFORD B., and G. PHELAN. "Australian Maritime Unions and Flag-of-Convenience Vessels." *Journal of Industrial Relations*. Forthcoming.

ECONOMIC AND SOCIAL COMMITTEE OF THE EUROPEAN COMMUNITIES. *EEC Shipping Policy—Flags of Convenience*. Brussels: Economic and Social Committee of the European Communities, 1979.

FAYLE, ERNEST C. *A Short History of the World's Shipping Industry*. London: Allen & Unwin, 1933.

FINGARD, JUDITH. *Jack in Port: Sailortowns in Eastern Canada*. Toronto: University of Toronto Press, 1982.

FLETCHER, BARBARA. "The Expansion of the Shipping Federation, 1906–1910." *Maritime Policy and Management* 11, no. 4 (1984).

FORSYTH, CRAIG J. "Sea Daddy: An Excursus into an Endangered Social Species." *Maritime Policy and Management* 13, no. 1 (1986).

FORSYTH, CRAIG J., and WILLIAM B. BANKSTON. "The Merchant Seaman as a Social Type: A Marginal Life-Style." *Free Inquiry in Creative Sociology* 11, no. 1 (1983).

———. "The Social Psychological Consequences of a Life at Sea." *Maritime Policy and Management* 11, no. 2 (1984).

FRICKE, PETER H. *Seafaring and Community: Towards a Social Understanding of Seafaring*. London: Croom Helm, 1973.

———. *The Social Structure of the Crews of British Dry Cargo Merchant Ships*. Cardiff: University of Wales Institute of Science & Technology, 1972.

GO, STELLA P., LETITIA T. POSTRADO, and PILAR RAMOS-

JIMENEZ. *The Effect of International Contract Labor.* Manila: Integrated Research Center, De la Salle University Press, 1983.

GOLD, EDGAR. *Maritime Transport: The Evolution of International Marine Policy and Shipping Law.* Lexington, Mass.: Lexington Books, 1981.

GOLDBERG, JOSEPH P. *The Maritime Story: A Study in Labor-Management Relations.* Cambridge: Harvard University Press, 1958.

GOLDING, KENNETH. *ITF: A Brief Survey of the History and Activities of the International Transport Workers' Federation.* Amsterdam: International Transport Workers' Federation, 1952.

GORTER, WYTZE, and GEORGE H. HILDEBRAND. *The Pacific Coast Maritime Shipping Industry, 1930–1948.* Berkeley: University of California Press, 1954.

GREEN, JIM. *Against the Tide: The Story of the Canadian Seamen's Union.* Toronto: Progress Books, 1986.

GREEN, REGINALD, ed. *The International Financial System: An Ecumenical Critique.* Geneva: World Council of Churches, 1984.

GREY, MICHAEL. *Changing Course: A Second Career for the Seafarers within the Maritime Industry.* London: Fairplay, 1980.

———. "Lookout." *Fairplay International Shipping Weekly*, Feb. 7, 1985.

———. "Lookout." *Fairplay International Shipping Weekly*, May 17, 1990.

GUEST, ANDREW. "Industry Ponders How to Raise Standards." *Seatrade*, Nov.-Dec. 1988.

HARLAND, SAMUEL J. *The Dustless Road.* Reading: Educational Explorers, 1965.

HEALY, JAMES C. *Fo'c'sle and Glory Holy: A Study of the Merchant Seaman and His Occupation.* New York: Merchant Marine Publishing Association, 1936.

HEATON, PAUL M. *The Redbook: A Deep Sea Tramp.* Risca, Wales: Starling Press, 1981.

HEATON, PHILIP. "A Trade Union View of Change in the Shipping Industry." Edinburgh: Scottish Academic Press, 1984.

HEMINGWAY, JOHN. *Conflict and Democracy: Studies in Trade Union Government.* Oxford: Clarendon Press, 1978.

HILL, J. M. M. *The Seafaring Career: A Study of the Forces Affecting Joining, Serving and Leaving the Merchant Navy.* London: Travistock Institute of Human Relations, 1972.

HODGES, SUSAN L. H., ed. *Legal Rights of Seafarers.* London: Nautical Institute, 1988.

HOGBEN, RICK. *A Sharp Look-out: One Hundred Years of Maritime History as Reported in* Fairplay. London: Fairplay, 1983.

HOHMAN, ELMO P. *History of American Merchant Seamen.* Hamden, Conn.: Shoe String Press, 1956.

———. *Seamen Ashore.* New Haven: Yale University Press, 1952.

———. "Work and Wages of American Merchant Seamen." *Industrial and Labor Relations Review* 15 (1962).

HOLDER, L. A., and DAVID H. MOREBY. "Technology and Manning for Safe Ship Operations in the 1990's." Privately published, 1988.

HOPE, REGINALD, ed. *Seamen's World.* London: Marine Society, 1982.

————. *Sea Pie*. London: Marine Society, 1984.

————. *Twenty Singing Seamen*. London: Marine Society, 1971.

HOPE, RONALD. *The Merchant Navy*. London: Standford Maritime, 1980.

HUNTER, GEORGE MCPHERSON. "Destitution among Seamen." *Survey*, Aug. 3, 1912.

HURD, ARCHIBALD. *The Triumph of the Tramp Ship*. London: Cassell, 1922.

INTERNATIONAL LABOR OFFICE. *Inspection of Labor Conditions on Board Ship: Guide Lines for Procedure*. Geneva: International Labor Office, 1990.

JONES, STEPHEN. "Early Seamen's Trade Unions on the Northeast Coast, 1784–1844." *Maritime History* 3, no. 1 (1973).

JOSUE, NOEL L., and PAUL A BUNIEL. *Bibliography on Philippine Seafarers and Shipping*. Manila: Maritime Education and Research Center, 1991.

JUNGBLUT, CHRISTIAN. "Need a License? Get One Cheap with Graft." *Log*, March 1981.

KAPLAN, WILLIAM. *Everything That Floats: Pat Sullivan, Hal Banks and the Seamen's Union of Canada*. Toronto: University of Toronto Press, 1987.

KILGOUR, JOHN G. *The United States' Merchant Marine: National Maritime Policy and Industrial Relations*. New York: Praeger, 1975.

KUECHLE, DAVID. *The Story of the Savannah: An Episode in Maritime Labor-Management Relations*. Cambridge: Harvard University Press, 1971.

LAMPMAN, ROBERT J. "Collective Bargaining of West Coast Sailors, 1885–1947." Ph.D. diss., University of Wisconsin, 1950.

LANE, TONY. *Grey Dawn Breaking*. Manchester: Manchester University Press, 1986.

————. *The Merchant Seamen's War*. Manchester: Manchester University Press, 1991.

LEBACK, WARREN G. *The Management of Safety in Shipping*. London: Nautical Institute, 1991.

LEMISCH, JESSE. "Jack Tar in the Streets: Merchant Seamen in the Politics of Revolutionary America." *William and Mary Quarterly* 24 (1968).

LLOYD, CHRISTOPHER. *The British Seaman, 1200–1860*. Rutherford, N.J.: Fairleigh Dickinson University Press, 1970.

LLOYD'S REGISTER. *Statistical Tables, 1990*. London: Lloyd's Register, 1990.

MCCONVILLE, J. *The Shipping Industry in the United Kingdom*. Geneva: International Institute of Labour Studies, 1977.

MCFEE, WILLIAM. *In the First Watch*. London: Faber and Faber, 1947.

MCKAY, RICHARD C. *South Street: A Maritime History of New York*. New York: G. P. Putnam's Sons, 1934.

MCPHEE, JOHN. *Looking for a Ship*. New York: Farrar, Straus & Giroux, 1990.

MAGDEN, RONALD, and A. D. MARTINSON. *The Working Waterfront: The Story of Tacoma's Ships and Men*. Tacoma, Wash.: International Longshoremen and Warehousemen's Union, Local 23, 1982.

MAGUIRE, JOHN MACARTHER. *The Lance of Justice*. Cambridge, Mass.: Harvard University Press, 1928.

MANNHEIM, BILHA F., and ELIEZER ROSENSTEIN. "Occupational Behavior and Commitment of Seamen." *Maritime Policy and Management* 3, no. 1 (1975).

MARINE TECHNOLOGY SOCIETY. *The Ocean: An International Workplace. Proceedings of a Conference*. Halifax: IEEE Ocean Engineering Society, 1987.

MARINE TRANSPORTATION RESEARCH BOARD. "Human Error in Merchant Marine Safety." Washington, D.C.: U.S. Department of Commerce, 1976.

MARSH, ARTHUR. *History of the National Union of Seamen in the United Kingdom*. Forthcoming.

MASON, MICHAEL, BASIL GREENHILL, and ROBIN CRAIG. *The British Seafarer*. London: Hutcheson, 1980.

MASTERS, DAVID. *The Plimsoll Mark*. London: Cassell, 1955.

MEIJER, FIK. *A History of Seafaring in the Classical World*. London: Croom Helm, 1986.

MINISTRY OF TRANSPORT AND CIVIL AVIATION. *Seafarers and Their Ships: The Story of a Century of Progress in the Safety of Ships and the Well-Being of Seamen*. New York: Philosophical Library, 1956.

MOORE, MICHAEL. *Container Ship: A Voyage on the Tolaga Bay*. London: Hamish Hamilton, 1986.

MOREBY, DAVID H. *The Human Element in Shipping*. Colchester: Seatrade, 1975.

—————. *Personnel Management in Merchant Shipping*. Oxford: Pergamon Press, 1986.

MORISON, SAMUEL ELIOT. *Maritime History of Massachusetts, 1783–1860*. Boston: Houghton Miflin, 1961.

NAESS, ERLING. *The Great PanLibHon Controversy*. Epping, Essex: Gower Press, 1972.

National Research Council. *Crew Size and Maritime Safety*. Washington, D.C.: National Academy Press, 1991.

- —————. *Effective Manning of the U.S. Merchant Fleet*. Washington, D.C.: National Academy Press, 1984.

NATIONAL UNION OF SEAMEN. *British Shipping: Heading for the Rocks: A Rescue Plan from the National Union of Seamen*. London: National Union of Seamen, 1982.

NAUTICAL INSTITUTE. "Safety and Employment—Are They Linked?" *Seaways*, June 1991.

NELSON, BRUCE. *Workers on the Waterfront—Seamen, Longshoremen, and Unionism in the 1930's*. Urbana: University of Illinois Press, 1990.

NOLAN, BRIAN. "Seamen, Drink and Social Structure." *Maritime Policy and Managment* 4, no. 2 (1976).

—————. "Triple Doses: A View of Seamen's Health." *Maritime Policy and Management* 6, no. 2 (1979).

NORRIS, MARTIN J. *The Law of Seamen*. Rochester, N.Y.: Lawyers' Cooperative Publishing, 1970.

NORTHRUP, HERBERT R., and RICHARD L. ROWAN. *The International Transport Workers' Federation and Flag of Convenience Shipping*. Philadelphia: Wharton School International Research Unit, 1983.

OMMER, ROSEMARY, and GERALD PANTING, eds. *Working Men Who Got Wet*. St. John's: Maritime History Group, Memorial University of Newfoundland, 1980.

OTTERLAND, ANDERS. *A Sociomedical Study of Mortality in Merchant Seafarers*. London: William Heinemann, 1960.

PALMER, SARAH, and GLYNDWR WILLIAMS. *Charted and Uncharted Waters*. Greenwich, England: National Maritime Museum, 1981.

PETERSON, GWENN B. *Careers in the United States Merchant Marine*. New York: E. P. Dutton, 1983.

PETRUCELLI, LINDA. "The Price of Fish on the Island of Taiwan." *Lookout*, Summer 1989.

POWELL, L. H. *The Shipping Federation: A History of the First Sixty Years, 1890–1950*. London: International Shipping Federation, 1950.

PUNEKAR, S. D. *The Socio-Economic Conditions of Indian Seaman and Their Welfare*. Bombay: Tata Institute of Social Services, 1977.

RADIOTELEVISIONE ITALIANA. *Ships to Sink (Navi con licenza d'affondare)*. Rome: Radiotelevisione Italiana, 1980.

RASKIN, BERNARD. *On a True Course: The Story of the National Maritime Union, AFL-CIO*. New York: National Maritime Union, 1967.

REDIKER, MARCUS. *Between the Devil and the Deep Blue Sea: Merchant Seamen, Pirates and the Anglo American Maritime World, 1700–1750*. Cambridge: Cambridge University Press, 1987.

REYNOLDS, BERTHA. *Unchartered Journey*. New York: Citadel Press, 1963.

ROBINSON, ROBERT B. *Of Whales and Men*. New York: Alfred Knopf, 1954.

ROCHDALE VISCOUNT. *Committee of Inquiry into Shipping*. London: Her Majesty's Stationery Office, 1970.

ROGGEMA, JACQUES. "The Design of Shipboard Organization: Some Experiences with a Matrix Type of Organization in Norway." *Maritime Policy and Management* 4, no. 5 (1977).

RUBIN, CHARLES. *The Log of Rubin the Sailor*. New York: International Publishers, 1973.

SADLER, JACK. *Discipline at Sea and Industrial Relations in the Shipping Industry*. Glasgow: Brown Son and Ferguson, 1983.

SAGER, ERIC. *Seafaring Labor: The Merchant Marine and Atlantic Canadians, 1820–1914*. Montreal: McGill-Queens University Press, 1989.

SAMUELS, SAMUEL. *From the Fo'c'sle to the Cabin*. New York: Harper, 1887.

SANGER, CLYDE. *Ordering the Oceans*. Toronto: University of Toronto Press, 1987.

SCARROT, TERRY. "Floating Coffins." *Seafarer*, New Year 1989.

SCHULTZ, CHARLES R. *Life on Board 19th-Century American Whalers*. College Station: Texas A & M University Press, 1987.

SCHURZ, WILLIAM LYTLE. *Manila Galleon*. Manila: Historical Society, 1985.

SHERAR, MIRIAM. *Shipping Out: A Sociological Study of American Merchant Seamen*. Cambridge, Md.: Cornell Maritime Press, 1973.

SHRANK, ROBERT. *Industrial Democracy at Sea: Authority and Democracy on a Norwegian Freighter*. Cambridge: MIT Press, 1983.

SMITH, COLIN V. D. "Trends and Patterns in Human Rights Violations at Sea." Master's thesis, Plymouth Polytechnic, 1983.

STANDARD, WILLIAM I. *Merchant Seamen: A Short History of Their Struggles*. New York: International Publishers, 1947.

STANTON, JOHN. *Life and Death of the Canadian Seamen's Union*. Toronto: Steel Rail, 1978.

STRAUSS, ROBERT. *Medical Care for Seamen*. New Haven: Yale University Press, 1950.

STURMEY, E. G. *British Shipping and World Competition*. London: Athlone Press, 1962.

SUNDBY, PER. "Occupation and Insanity." *Acta Psychiatrica et Neurologica Scandinavia*, 1955.

TALAMPAS, ROLANDO. *International Seafarers' Code: A Compendium of ILO Conventions and Resolutions for Seafarers*. Manila: Maritime Education and Research Center, 1991.

———. *Marino: An Introduction to the History of Filipino Seamen*. Manila: Maritime Education and Research Center, 1991.

———. "Seafarer Intellectuals." *Asia Seafarer*, Sept.-Oct. 1990.

TAYLOR, PAUL S. *The Sailors' Union of the Pacific*. New York: Ronald Press, 1923.

UNCTAD SECRETARIAT. *Review and Analysis of Possible Measures to Minimize the Occurrence of Maritime Fraud and Piracy*. Geneva: UNCTAD Secretariat, 1983.

U.S. MARITIME COMMISSION. *Economic Survey of the American Merchant Marine*. Washington, D.C.: Government Printing Office, 1937.

VILLAR, ROGER. *Piracy Today*. London: Conway Maritime, 1986.

WADA, K. *The Progress and Future Prospects of Modernization of the Manning System in Japan*. Tokyo: Japan Maritime Research Institute, 1986.

WADE, STEWART. "American Pie." *Fairplay International Shipping Weekly*, March 14, 1991.

WALL, M. R. "Job Satisfaction and Personality of Merchant Navy Officers." *Maritime Policy and Management* 7, no. 3 (1980).

WEINTRAUB, HYMAN. *Andrew Furuseth: Emancipator of the Seamen*. Berkeley: University of California Press, 1959.

WHITEHURST, CLINTON H., JR. *The U.S. Merchant Marine: In Search of an Enduring Maritime Policy*. Annapolis, Md.: Naval Institute Press, 1983.

WILSON, J. HAVELOCK. *My Stormy Voyage through Life*. London: Cooperative Printing Society, 1925.

WINTHER, ROSALYN. "Serving a Sentence out at Sea." *Seatrade*, March 1985.

SELECTED FICTION

CONRAD, JOSEPH. *Lord Jim*. 1900. Reprint. New York: Harcourt Brace Jovanovich, 1980.

————. *Mirror of the Sea*. 1906. Reprint. New York: Harcourt Brace Jovanovich, 1980.

————. *Nigger of the Narcissus*. 1897. Reprint. New York: Harcourt Brace Jovanovich, 1980.

————. *Typhoon*. 1903. Reprint. New York: Harcourt Brace Jovanovich, 1980.

————. *Youth*. 1902. Reprint. New York: Harcourt Brace Jovanovich, 1980.

HANLEY, JAMES. *Between the Tides*. London: Methuen, 1939.

————. *Broken Water*. London: Chatto and Windus, 1937.

————. *Hollow Sea*. London: John Lane, 1938.

LONDON, JACK. *Sea Wolf*. New York: Macmillan, 1904.

LOWRY, MALCOLM. *Ultramarine*. 1933. Reprint. Middlesex: Penguin, 1962.

MELVILLE, HERMAN. *Moby Dick*. New York: G. P. Putnam and Sons, 1892.

————. *White Jacket*. London: Russell & Russell, 1963.

O'NEILL, EUGENE. *The Long Voyage Home: Seven Plays of the Sea*. 1919. Reprint. New York: Modern Library, 1946.

REINER, LARRY. *Minute of Silence*, Phoenix, Ariz.: Integra Press, 1990.

INDEX